Handbook of Reporting and Communication Skills

[Revised and Enlarged Edition]

ABOUT THE AUTHORS

VS Gupta, a senior media and communication academic, is a former Professor at Haryana Agricultural University, Hisar. A recipient of several awards and fellowships, Professor Gupta conceptualised and implemented a number of training programmes in journalism and communication at the university.

As the Country Representative for the Asian Media Information and Communication Centre (AMIC), Singapore, for a number of years, he organised numerous seminars and colloquia on various aspects of the media throughout the country. He has written and edited, jointly and singly, nine books and a number of manuals, besides having been widely published in India and abroad.

Rahul Kumar is a journalist and a communications professional. He has worked as a journalist with The Times of India, The Pioneer, The Financial Express, The Asian Age and India Today. As a Reporter he has covered national and state elections, written on urban development as well as health and environmental issues. Rahul has also written for India's national broadcaster, All India Radio, on foreign affairs and international issues.

He has worked in the international development sector as a communications professional and has written news and features on various issues from the US, China, UK, Italy, Nepal, Brazil, Spain and other countries.

He was awarded the Chevening fellowship by the UK's Foreign, Commonwealth and Development Office (FCDO); has undergone training programmes by the Thomson Reuters Foundation in New York and by Radio Netherlands Training Centre in the Netherlands.

Handbook of Reporting and Communication Skills

[Revised and Enlarged Edition]

V.S. Gupta
Rahul Kumar

CONCEPT PUBLISHING COMPANY PVT. LTD.
NEW DELHI-110059

ISBN: 978-93-5594-531-0 (HB)

ISBN: 978-93-5594-532-7 (PB)

First Published 2003
Revised and Enlarged Edition 2023

Published and Printed by

Concept Since 1974

Concept Publishing Company Pvt. Ltd.
A/15-16, Commercial Block, Mohan Garden,
New Delhi-110059 (India)
T: +91 11 41101460
E: publishing@conceptpub.com, *W*: www.conceptpub.com

Cataloging in Publication—Courtesy: D.K. Agencies (P) Ltd. <docinfo@dkagencies.com>

Gupta, V. S., author.
Handbook of reporting and communication skills / V.S. Gupta, Rahul Kumar. -- Revised and enlarged edition.
pages cm
Includes bibliographical references and index.
ISBN 9789355945310 (HB)
ISBN 9789355945327 (PB)

1. Reporters and reporting--India. 2. Communication--India. I. Kumar, Rahul (Journalist), author. II. Title.

LCC PN4781.G87 2023 | DDC 070.430954 23

Preface

The authors of the companion volume of this book, *Handbook of Journalism and Mass Communication*, had promised to bring out separately another publication incorporating practical aspects of journalism—reporting, sub-editing and newspaper production. Here is, therefore, the publication designed for the students of journalism, and all others interested in improving their writing and communication skills.

The book has been written in a reader-friendly manner. In most of the chapters—checklists, guidelines, tips, and dos and don'ts, and examples have been given in the hope that these will become a part of practice for the students. Efforts have also been made to acquaint the readers with the nuances of the changing trends in journalism. Most of the examples given are from a large number of newspapers and magazines, mostly Indian. The recurring emphasis is on improving the quality of language, which is fast becoming a casualty in contemporary journalism.

No claims, however, are made or intended that merely by purchasing this book, a student will be joining the finishing school of journalism. The practical aspects of journalism, communication skills, document designing and technical writing can be learnt only through actual practice. In India, it is mostly on the shop floor of newspapers. The book is only an aid to entry in the profession. It would, however, be pertinent to heed the advice given in the book: *No amount of theorizing about the principles and techniques of news reporting and editing will help you without hands-on practice. The effort will be futile, just like trying to learn swimming without getting wet.*

While writing this book, as in our earlier publication, I have tried to use all the good knowledge on the subject. The publications brought out by AMIC, FES, PII, IIMC and PCI have been a great source of knowledge and information. My association with the two apex institutions in the area of journalism and mass communication, AMIC and PII have been particularly rewarding.

The PII, this year, is completing 40 years of its existence. Its two periodicals, *Vidura* and *Grassroots* are the examples of all that is good in journalism. Thousands of journalists and journalism teachers, like me have been greatly benefited from the activities, training programmes and publications of PII. This calls for felicitations to the institution and its Director, Mr. Ajit Bhattacharjee, and the staff, who have given so much to the world of journalism.

Suggestions for improvement of the book, are welcome and shall be incorporated in the forthcoming editions.

V.S. Gupta

Preface to the Revised Edition

The book, *Handbook of Reporting and Communication Skills*, has been revised for the first time since its publication in 2003. During this period the media scenario has witnessed far reaching changes. The global media finds itself faced with new challenges while the Indian media finds itself on the threshold of a credibility crisis. Media consumers have become producers while journalists find themselves under pressure from the masses and governments. Fast-evolving technology continues to disrupt media processes and forces journalists and media practitioners to grow and experiment.

To keep up with the latest changes and trends in media and communication, the author of this book, Prof. V.S. Gupta has sought the good offices of Delhi-based journalist and communications expert Rahul Kumar to revise the book. This first revised edition introduces numerous practical aspects of journalism that students will find useful in their field work. Every chapter of the book has been updated with revised information and fresh examples. New information has been added to the chapters on News Organisation and Reporting.

The chapter on Information Technology has been overhauled to give an insight into the evolution of the internet, websites and online journalism. The new chapter looks at the impact of digital technologies on journalists as well as the consumers of media. We have the latest perspective on the use of social media platforms along with the rise of fake news.

A new chapter on Magazine Journalism has been added as magazines have witnessed a major transformation in the last two decades. Dozens of niche and lifestyle magazines have hit the stands bringing a variety of content to a highly diversified readership.

Amidst all these developments, one fundamental which has not changed is that students, who aspire to be journalists or communicators, still remain the primary readers for this book. However, they have witnessed one change—their sources of scholarship and learning have moved on from libraries, books, teachers, parents and peers to also include Google, internet and smart phones. It is not a surprise to see students jabbing furiously at their smart phones during the class just to verify the information given by the teacher.

One important aspect of this book is that the readers will be able to visualise the transformation that has taken place in the media industry and the field of journalism during the last two decades. We hope that the book retains its value at a time when all kinds of information can be downloaded from the internet. We also hope that the revised *Handbook of Reporting and Communication Skills* will add knowledge to the student-readers which they find useful during their professional careers.

V.S. Gupta
Rahul Kumar

Contents

Introduction

In the Midst of the Knowledge Revolution

The current generation is lucky to be born in the midst of the Fourth Industrial Revolution, often called the Knowledge Revolution. The interesting fact is every activity that today's humans do over internet, smart phones and social media, they are in some ways contributing to advancing the knowledge revolution. So, what exactly is the **Knowledge Revolution**? Simply put it is internet along with various new age technologies that are coming together and building knowledge for individual and human progress. The Fourth Industrial Revolution is building itself on the Third Industrial Revolution, also called the Digital Revolution, that had begun in the middle of the last century kickstarted by the convergence of the computer and the internet.

Just visualise it—even if you do not want a copy of the daily newspaper thrown into your home every morning, you can still read it on your mobile. You do not agree with the editor's opinion about the environment policy, you can tweet your opinion and tag the editor. If you are perturbed about what a reporter has written, you do not sit back helpless like in earlier times. You send your opinion to the reporter and also put in on Facebook and LinkedIn. You are into photography but do not have to go searching for a publication to take your photographs. You make your own website or upload your photographs on Instagram and reach out to the world. You don't have the means to appear on a TV channel or in a film, record your own video and upload it on YouTube. Everything is so simple and inexpensive. Earlier, to seek answers you had to speak to an expert or visit the library but now you simply '**Google it**.'

In this revolution, which is currently unfolding before our eyes, we see that the world of media has been completely disrupted by technology. Let us look at this from another angle. If earlier we only had journalists as the producers of news and information, now we have the masses doing almost the same thing. The people across the country are producing, creating and generating photographs, write-ups and content round the clock. At the same time, millions of Indians are also reading this content, replying to it, sharing it and spreading it further. We have also seen the rise of the **citizen reporter** after many media outlets allowed people to send information and photographs to them. The knowledge revolution has had a far-reaching impact on every sector, including on the media. Such massive disruption in the media industry is catalysing a change in a country of subcontinental dimensions, with a linguistic and culturally diverse population of around 1.3 billion that thinks in such multi-hued ways.

Despite the social media platforms and communication of information through mobile phone-based groups, the mainstream media continues to play a vital role in building public opinion by way of disseminating trustworthy information to the people. Even now news, fearless editorial criticism and in-depth articles in newspapers and magazines influence governance in the country. Today, people have access to a wide range of publications, published in different languages with various periodicities and catering to diverse interests, virtually at their doorsteps.

Indian Media Landscape

India is one of the few large countries which continues to see growth in the print media industry. Even as a significant number of well-established newspapers across the world are closing down their print editions, or reducing their printed copies, while maintaining their presence in the online space, the Indian print media continues to flourish in regional languages, Hindi and English. However, not all of this growth has been uniform. There have been challenges in other spheres. News magazines are facing difficult times even as niche and special magazines seem to be doing well.

Indian Media at a Glance in 2018

		Numbers
1.	Total publications	1,18,239
2.	Newspapers	17,573
3.	Periodicals	1,00,666
4.	Hindi language has the largest number of publications	47,989
5.	English language has the second-largest number of publications	14,626
6.	Dainik Bhaskar with 58 editions is the largest circulated multi-edition daily	51,19,720
7.	The Times of India, with 34 editions is the second-largest circulated multi-edition daily	43,34,769
8.	Homes with a TV set	19,70,00,000
9.	TV Channels uplinked from India	797
10.	TV Channels uplinked from abroad	84
11.	Total mobile subscribers	1,17,60,00,000
12.	Broadband subscribers	51,85,50,000

Notes

- Figures 1-7 from the website of Registrar of Newspapers for India http://rni.nic.in/all_page/press_india.aspx
- Figure 8 from Broadcast India 2018 survey by Broadcast Audience Research Council https://www.barcindia.co.in/resources/pdf/BARC%20India%20Universe%20Update%20-%202018.pdf
- Figures 9-10 from the website of the Telecom Regulatory Authority of India https://main.trai.gov.in/sites/default/files/RecommendationUL25062018.pdf
- Figures 11 and 12 from the website of the Telecom Regulatory Authority of India https://main.trai.gov.in/sites/default/files/PR_No.101of2019.pdf

The Indian press, by far still the freest press in South Asia, continues to be largely urban-oriented. This is true of the newspapers that are published from the metros. Despite the massive changes in the media space, the English press continues to cater to an elite audience, geared to commercial culture and obsessed with garnering the maximum share of advertising revenue. Issues concerning rural development continue to fight for adequate coverage. On the other hand, the readers of the Indian language press include the widest spectrum from first generation readers to political leaders and many sections of people in between.

With the media continuing to grow in India, it has a catalytic role to play in enhancing development and contributing to the social and economic welfare of people. Issues related to women, education, water, health and agriculture still constitute the anchor of our development programmes.

In every country, newspapers cater to a wide range of readership. For example, let us look at an old snippet about the newspapers in England.

The Times—Read by people who run the country.

Daily Mirror—Read by people who think they run country.

The Guardian—Read by people who think they ought to run the country.

The Morning Star—Read by people who think the country ought to be run by another country.

Daily Mail—Read by the wives of the people who run the country.

Financial Times—Read by people who own the country.

Daily Express—Read by people who think the country ought to be run as it used to be.

The Daily Telegraph—Read by people who think it is run.

Shifting Sands

Today's knowledge revolution has been built over smaller technology revolutions that happened over the last four decades. During the closing decades of the twentieth century, the media landscape underwent a complete metamorphosis. Satellite television was one of these which created a new cultural market, transcending national boundaries and acquiring geopolitical significance. The technologies, tools, methods and formats of news gathering, presentation and analysis changed. The monopoly of state owned Doordarshan and All India Radio was largely eroded due to the exponential growth of Indian and foreign TV channels. Media consumers—the newspaper readers, radio audience and the television viewers have become more discerning and therefore, more demanding.

Now, the logic of 24 hours television means that every move, every soundbyte, is transmitted to millions of viewers in a matter of minutes. Political leaders, experts and television commentators are becoming more and more TV savvy. The young television reporters and anchors of the 24 hours news channels have the star value thrust on them overnight.

It was, of course, premised that with the ongoing trends of globalization and opening up of the economy, the market forces would be a major determining factor in shaping the contours of media. As globalization began to open the eyes of Indians to foreign and Western media influences, the media began to get more commercialised, and more frivolous. An increasing number of newspapers started special sections on the P3P circuit to the exclusion of news in other important areas. Models, fashion designers, actors and actresses, society persons and socialites—all the people from the cocktail circuit. To a young and a not so discerning reader, it would appear that all that is happening in the capital city is wining, dining, dancing and dating.

Looking into the Future

One of the challenges confronting the contemporary society is: how to cope with the rapid-fire technological, economic and geopolitical changes; as well as the changes in the social and development sector. The term 'change' has in fact become the defining attribute of the closing decades of the 20th century and the first two decades of the 21st century. In the knowledge revolution, ideas and information have become power. It is already beginning to change perceptions, induce paradigm shift in concepts and theories and transform even well-established systems.

In a matter of just a few decades, we have leapfrogged from the relentless advance of the Information Revolution, to the Knowledge Revolution. Interestingly, this has been an important contributory factor in encouraging and strengthening the forces of globalization. Online and mobile news platforms allow consumers to understand breaking news and events in a personalized context that makes better sense to them. It also helps them to build new communities based on common interests and share all of that information, something impossible in any other medium. This was an element that we realised had a negative side to it—it enabled the masses to share and spread fake news and misinformation that would go viral within hours. The quantity of content is so enormous that a seeker of information often has to spend an inordinate amount of time sifting the right information from the wrong one. If the knowledge revolution has provided information to people at their fingertips, it has also led to the generation of copious amounts of wrong information.

The Best of Times, the Worst of Times: Charles Dickens, in the opening lines of his famous novel, *A Tale of Two Cities* says: It was the best of times, it was the worst of times, it was the age of wisdom, it was the age off foolishness, it was the epoch of belief, it was the epoch of incredulity, it was the season of light, it was the season of darkness, it was the spring of hope, it was the winter of despair, we had everything before us, we had nothing before us.

Likewise, when we look at the contemporary society, and the social, political and economic settings, we find ourselves confronted with a host of new concepts some of which are: *Future Shock*, *The End of History*, *Third Wave*, *Death of Distance*, *Clash of Civilizations*, *Knowledge Society* and many more. More than the titles of the books these terms encapsulate in themselves ideas, concepts and analysis of trends in the 'global village'; that the world is fast becoming. All these concepts represent emerging social and political directions in the modern society, which would perhaps be known as the most productive period in terms of ideas, paradigms and thoughts.

Welcome to the world of Ideas.
Welcome to the Knowledge Revolution.

NOTE

1. P.P. Singh Memorial Lecture delivered by Shri H.Y. Sharda Prasad, Information Adviser to Prime Minister, on 8 September, 1992.

1

Developing Communication Skills

Fundamentals of Good Writing

A journalist is essentially a communicator. He communicates through words—written as well as spoken. Words are the basic component of a language. It is, therefore, imperative that a journalist is fairly competent to understand the essentials of a language clearly, fluently and with confidence. Without a good grounding and proficiency in the language, it would be futile to expect to do well in journalism.

Journalism is a craft with established rules, procedures and guidelines, as well as techniques and deadlines. Besides several other qualities—quite demanding by themselves—a journalist has to have a flair for language and the urge to communicate in words. Such a flair or talent for language may not be inborn. In such a situation, mastery over the language needs to be cultivated through hard work, diligence and single-minded effort over a period of time.

This chapter will acquaint you with some of the essentials of developing communication skills needed to become a journalist. We do not propose to take up the basics of grammar here because it is understood that a journalist, even at the training stage, would have been familiar with it, having studied it at the university level. We will, however, discuss the fundamentals of good writing, which will go a long way in evolving your own style of writing in due course.

Fundamentals of Good Writing

1. All Good Journalists and Writers are Avid Readers

Reading, as an activity and a habit, cultivated over a period of time, will always be found to be a rewarding preoccupation. In any case, reading not only strengthens your vocabulary and improves your language but is absolutely essential for getting ideas. At times, reading is inspirational. Reading also helps develop a style. Who has not been benefited by reading classics by old masters—Shakespeare and Charles Dickens or our own writers—Gandhi and Jawaharlal Nehru? All of them have enriched the language and come to our rescue whenever we look for a memorable phrase. Some of their memorable ideas and phrases are quoted so often that at times we wonder as to whether we would be able to use English without referring to the writings of these great masters. As illustrations, I would restrict myself to only one such reference from each of them:

Shakespeare

> *What a piece of work is a man!*
> *How noble in reason!*
> *How infinite in faculty!*
> *In form, in moving, how express and admirable!*
> *In action, how like an angel!*
> *In apprehension, how like a god!* (Hamlet)

Charles Dickens

> *It was the best of times, it was the worst of times, it was the age of wisdom, it was the age of foolishness.*
> *It was the epoch of belief, it was the epoch of incredulity, it was the season of Light, it was the season of Darkness, it was the spring of hope, it was the winter of despair.*
> (A Tale of Two Cities)

Reading should not be confined to the classics or great writers. Important magazines and newspapers, including niche publications should be the other essential reading for a journalist. It furnishes you with a storehouse of memorable occasions and interesting anecdotes. It helps improve language and gives ideas. Reading, therefore, is an essential prerequisite for developing communication skills. Good communicators and writers are life-long readers. They collect story ideas from whatever they read.

2. *Writing an Act of Faith, not a Trick of Grammar—The Elements of Style*

The remarks by William Strunk and E.B. White, the authors of the above book, constitute the core of the writing process. A writer, and even a reporter, has to have faith in himself and in his ability to work long hours, sometimes for years together, consistently over an extended period of time. According to Roy Peter Clark, who may be the best-known writing coach in the United States, and served in that capacity at the *St. Petersburg Times* for two years, "immersing themselves" in the story is one of the fourteen traits of good writers. They live it, breathe it and dream it. That, writing is no 9-5 office job is accepted by writers, reporters and journalists. While the romantic notion of a writer waiting for "inspiration" to dawn and guide him through his much-cherished writing project has always appeared to be fanciful, writing involves consistent hard work all through. And that spirit of working hard and long would not be forthcoming if the writer does not have faith in himself. A thorough knowledge of language and felicity of expression would certainly assist the writer through the process of writing. These would be no substitute for faith, which alone sustains the writer. A writer continuously reaffirms the faith in himself and in his craft of writing through consistent effort just as a performer does in case of music and dance through *sadhna* and *riaz* for the perfection of his art over long hours for months and years.

In this context, Irmscher has made a valid observation: Writing is a complex form of behaviour. It involves your mind, your senses and your feeling as well as your hands. Writing involves the whole self.

3. *A Basic Structural Design is Essential for Writing*

Most of the outstanding scholars who have guided generations of writers and reporters, are unanimously of the view that a basic structural design underlines every kind of writing. Strunk and White say: Writing to be effective must follow closely the thoughts of the writer, but not necessarily in the order in which the thoughts occur. This calls for a scheme of procedure. In most cases, planning must precede writing. The first principle of composition is to foresee or determine the shape of what is to come and pursue that shape. The more clearly the writer perceives the shape, the better are the chances of success. Adequate preparation, organisation and analysis of data would help you achieve clarity in thinking. This will further enhance your efficiency towards successful completion of the project.

Plan your writing clearly in your thoughts. Several writers term this step—organising the material, which includes information, data and notes, as an exploratory work. The exploratory work has been sometimes frustratingly called 'mechanical drudgery'. It would, however, be important to emphasise that upon the diligence put in this hackwork would largely depend the quality of your publication.

Roy Peter Clark, in his article in *Washington Journalism Review*, developed a list of fourteen traits often shared by good writers. One of the essential traits is planning as an important part of writing. Search for relevant literature and references constitute an essential part of organising the project. A writer has to spend a great deal of time in conducting a literature review that would also include a study of his own previous writings.

4. Language for Reporting

The most important element in the process of writing is the language. In this section, we shall discuss some of the principles of writing, which a journalist will do well to remember and practice. Some of these may appear to be elementary, nonetheless these are important.

The style of news reporting has to be plain, simple and in a practical form. Newspaper reports are read and understood by a cross-section of readership—people from a variety of educational backgrounds and cultures. Newspaper language, therefore, has to be simple and straightforward. Some of the noteworthy aspects of newspaper language are listed below:

(a) Short Words, Short Sentences, Short Paragraphs

German philosopher Schopenhauer wrote: To use many words to

communicate few thoughts is everywhere the unmistakable sign of mediocrity.

Harold Evans, formerly editor of *The Times*, London, and one of the best English editors, says: Journalists should strive to use simple words which everyone can understand. In his book, *Newman's English*, he gives some examples of how writing with words that ordinary people use not only shortens the message but makes the message interesting and intelligible.

Here is an example: *We are all aware of the significant need to maintain uppermost in the mind of mankind the stark need of avoiding bloody international conflict. One method by which this can be nurtured is to revive the solemn aspect of the great aspect of life, which has resulted from such catastrophic struggles within the theatres of war.*

Evans edits this down to: *Men need reminding of the horrors of war. One way to do this is to honour those who died.*

In this context, it will be difficult to improve upon the advice given by Strunk and White:

> A sentence should contain no unnecessary words, a paragraph no unnecessary sentences, for the same reason that a drawing should have no unnecessary lines and a machine no unnecessary parts. This requires not that the writers make all sentences short, or avoid all details and treat subjects only in outline, but that every word tells.

It is, therefore, necessary to omit needless words:

Avoid	**Prefer**
The question as to whether	Whether
There is no doubt but that	No doubt (doubtless)
Used for fuel purposes	Used for fuel
He is a man who	He
In a hasty manner	Hastily
The reason why is that	Because
Owing to the fact that	Since (because)
Call your attention to the fact that	Remind you

It is also essential to avoid what has been termed as "long-windedness".

Avoid	Prefer
Ahead of schedule	Early
At the present time	Now
Made an approach to	Approached
Put in an appearance	Appeared
Take into consideration	Consider
Submitted his resignation	Resigned
To voice approval	Approval

Equally important is to avoid circumlocution—a way of saying or writing something using more words than are necessary, instead of being clear or direct. Some examples:

Circumlocutions	Preferred Equivalents
Is dependent upon	Depends on
Was responsive to	Responded

(b) Prefer Familiar Words to Unfamiliar Ones, Short Words to Long Words

George Orwell, in *Politics and the English Language*, sets forth several rules. One of these is—never use a long word where a short one will do. Another advice is: "Do not use too many unfamiliar words together. Do not try to create an impression of being pompous. For example: Grave improprieties in his fiscal management, for irregularities in spending.

Original sentence/phrase	Revised sentence/phrase
The procurement of a quality bicycle warrants some forethought.	Buying a good bicycle requires forethought.
Organised labour has engendered a better life to many Americans.	Organised labour has given many Americans a better life.

Contemplating the purchase of...	Thinking of buying this...
This stems from the fact that...	This is because...

(c) Eliminate Clichés, Jargon and Bureaucratise

Writers should use words and phrases commonly understood by most of the people.

Clichés: The *Collins Cobuild Dictionary* defines clichés as an idea or phrase which has been used so much that it is no longer interesting or effective or, no longer has much meaning. Because of its accessibility, it also tends to be overused language. The cliché is a mark of tired and tried style. Some of the clichés commonly used are: All walks of life, part and parcel, food for thought, discuss threadbare, make hay while the sun shines, pot calling the kettle black, a straw in the wind, blow by blow, crying need, last but not the least, over and above, matters of life and death and many more. Reporters should be on alert and spot the clichés in their copy before handing their story in.

Jargon: Jargon is the inside talk understood mainly by those who are insiders. Insiders are members of a profession, they are specialists; like doctors, architects, NGO workers and others from a certain professional community. In case the report is meant for a specialist readership, then the use of jargon is in order. In this case the journalist need not unnecessarily strain at trying to explain each and every technical word. On the contrary, if the report is intended for a lay person, the technical terms will have to be defined.

Bureaucratise: Bureaucratise is a general name for a serious misuse of language. It is also called officialese. One writer calls officialese 'the cancer of language'. The translation of such language into everyday words is essential. It is the job of the reporter to make meaning clear to the readers. Let us look at some examples:

A major multinational company described sacking of staff after the closure of several factories as—"Volume related production schedule adjustment".

During the Gulf war, the fact that many Baghdad civilians were being killed by allied bombing was hidden behind the military phrase, "collateral damage".

These examples are surely an attempt to obscure and confuse people in an effort to hide the truth. Another example is "domiciliary unit", instead of a house. If 'officialeses' abound and clichés are used with abandon, can verbosity be far behind.

Frank Barton says the following about budget speeches:

> Budget speeches are a typical example of the way that important news is often wrapped-up in blankets of verbosity. Reporters should strip bare all the clichés with which most speeches are impregnated, "the arising out of", "for the purpose", "as a matter of fact". There are dozens more and they should never appear in newspapers.

(d) Keep the Writing Direct and Specific and Use Concrete Words

Good writing demands that our writing should be direct and specific and we use concrete words. A noteworthy advice in this context is:

> Prefer the specific to the general, the definite to the vague, the concrete to the abstract. The surest way to arouse and hold the readers' interest is being specific, definite and concrete.

A sentence like, 'it rained everyday for a week, is preferable to 'a period of unfavourable weather set in'.

Vagueness leads to inadvertent comment or value judgment. An interesting example is given by M.V. Kamath when he was summoned by his editor S. Natarajan, who asked him to explain what he meant by describing a man as elderly. This conversation goes on like this:

"Young man, how old is elderly?"

"Sir, the man in the story is forty-two."

"Well, I am elderly and I do not consider that I am elderly at all. I suggest you stick to giving the man's age and leave it at that. Let's have no more editorializing in copy."

Another examples of value judgment are the phrases, 'a massive audience' and 'a well-attended public meeting'. The question that such phrases would naturally raise: How exactly a massive audience would measure? Ten thousand? Fifty thousand? And, again what would a well-attended meeting would mean.

Two examples of direct writing are:

> He took a critical position on the President's budget.
> Her statements had the result of antagonizing the committee.

Alternatives:

> He criticized the President's budget.
> Her statements antagonized the committee.

(e) Word Economy

One major principle which all the journalists are enjoined to remember and practice is word economy. It saves space and also imparts clarity and precision to the expression. In this context, a manual for journalists has this to say:

> It is part of the skill of the journalist to be able to communicate effectively to everyone who reads the paper, listens to the radio or watches television. News stories must be clear, concise and easy to understand. Yet almost every newspaper in the world wastes space by using words and phrases, which are unnecessary, meaningless, complicated or repetitive.

Good writing demands that we eliminate this wasteful language for the following three reasons:

- The shortest expression is the clearest. It will be easily understood and will have maximum impact.
- It will save space for more facts and communicate extra information.
- Brevity and clarity help create a style, which is easy to read and hold attention.

It means that news writers must use words that are simple and clear, and convey meaning in an unambiguous way. We cannot afford to waste space in newspapers by using words that are unnecessary and meaningless.

Also delete useless modifiers. There is only one unique in the world. Pretty unique, very unique, almost unique, therefore, do not make any sense. The word 'very' is so overused that its meaning has been lost. Similarly, do not use 'very significant'; significant serves the purpose as well.

5. *Revise and Rewrite*

Revising the story is essential, reviewing is not enough. This is an advice you could ignore only at your peril. Another observation—rewriting usually makes the difference between a mediocre and a good write-up.

While working on a book, researching the topic is the first essential. The process of drafting and writing is considered as the next stage; and revising and proof-reading the other stage. In actual practice, however, revision goes on constantly in the writing process. Revising your draft also affords you an opportunity to refine and improve your writing, allowing you to restructure the sentences, eliminate repetition, remove overused words, cut down jargon and re-word awkward phrasing.

6. *A Check-list for Avoiding Poor Writing*

Avoid the following writing problems:

- Long sentences
- Long paragraphs or paragraphs with more than two topics
- Confusing wording
- Excessive jargon
- Words that readers may not understand and are not explained
- Ponderous, long and meaningless quotations, particularly from government and bureaucrats
- Statements in interviews or speeches that are not attributed
- Words that could be interpreted by readers in more than one way

- Trite phrases
- Misspelt words, words incorrectly used, grammatical issues.

REFERENCES

Bruce D. Itule and Douglas A. Anderson (1994): *News Writing and Reporting for Today's Media*, McGraw-Hill, Inc., New York.

Geoffrey Harris and David Spark (1997): *Practical Newspaper Reporting*, Focal Press.

Gregory A. Barnes (1986): *Write for Success*, ISI Press, Philadelphia.

William F. Irmscher (1981): *The Holt Guide to English*, Holt Rinehart and Winston, New York.

William Strunk and E.B. White (1999): *The Elements of Style*, Allyn and Bacon.

2

News

Nature and Structure

News means different things to different people. One of the definitions is, "newly received information or noteworthy information, especially about recent events." Some other definitions are:

News is information that is published in newspapers, in the online media and broadcast on radio and television about recent events in the world or in a particular area of activity.

News is sometimes used in the name of newspapers, for example, the *New York Daily News*. A well known daily newspaper published from Pakistan is *The News*. The newspaper was in news after the resignation of its editor facing undue pressure from the Pakistan government in covering the murder of American journalist Daniel Pearl.

If you say that someone or something is news, you mean that they are considered to be interesting and important, and that people want to hear about them on the radio, television, and read about them on the internet and in newspapers.

The operating words in the above examples are: information, newspapers, internet, radio, television, new events, interesting, important and people. Some other words associated with news are: bulletin, communiqué, dispatch, newsflash, statement and story.

So, the connotations of news are: information about recent events, which should be interesting and important. Story is another word used for news, like news story, feature story, or a reporter talking to another journalist: "Have you filed your story?"

Definitions

William Randolph Hearst: News is something someone somewhere wants suppressed. All the rest is advertising (i.e. news = disclosure).
Anonymous: News is the difference between the world yesterday and the world today. News is life; what is going on all-around us. News is what is reported.
Charles Dana, Editor, *New York Sun*: (a) News is anything which interests a large part of the community and which has never been brought to their attention. (b) Anything that will make the people talk.

Some More Definitions

News is what interests a good newspaperman.

—Gerald Johnson, *The Sun*, Baltimore

News is anything you did not know yesterday.

—Turner Catledge

Anything timely that interests a number of persons and best news is that which has the greatest interest for the greatest number.

—Williard G. Bleyer, in his textbook *Newspaper Writing and Editing*

In Williard G. Bleyer's definition, all the ingredients of news are encompassed.

Timely: Suggests that it is new, not previously known, an event of today, or late yesterday, or the latest angle to some earlier discussion.

Interest: The most important word in the definition, it suggests curiosity and concern.

Number: Suggests the vastness of readership of all kinds and that the newspaper is published for all classes and its scope is universal.

A newspaper differs from other types of publications by its immediacy, characteristics, headlines and coverage of a number of topical issues and events. According to the Royal Commission on the Press in Great Britain, to qualify as news, "an event must be first interesting to the public, and the public for this purpose means for each paper the people who read that paper."

Elements of News

A good news story has one or more of the following elements:

Timeliness: Time is the most important element in a news story. The news has to be new. However, today news has become almost instantaneous, with breaking news becoming the norm. The news about the attack on the Indian Parliament on 13 December, 2001 reached the nation in real time… as the action was happening. Of course, there was another reason for this—since the Parliament was in session, print and television journalists were already present there in full strength.

Just a few months earlier, the news about the attack on the World Trade Centre (WTC) in New York on 11 September, 2001 got around the world even as the event was happening.

The longest time gap in communications these days is human delay—and that too is being drastically reduced with the help of technological intervention.

Proximity: It is only natural that most of us are more interested in events in our own community and immediate surroundings than in some other place. Events in our own town are generally of greater interest to us than in a town 50 km away. Newspapers cast their news net around the area in which they are published. A typical news consumer is interested in familiar faces and familiar places. In other words, a local news incident which happens in the immediate neighbourhood, within a community, is of maximum interest to both—the reader as well as the newspaper or the TV Channel.

Sometimes, the event may happen far away, but have a direct relation with the local area. For example, if a local girl wins the Miss World Contest, the implication of the event, although not held locally has direct relevance to the local population.

Importance: Generally speaking the importance of a news story speaks for itself. The reporter rarely has to make much of a judgment about it and is only supposed to report the story. The election of Barack Obama as the first black president of the US in 2007-08 was a story of global significance and, therefore, reported widely across the world.

Conflict: Whatever be the dimensions, conflict—man against man, nation against nation, disagreements, arguments, battles—have been major topics for news reporting. Conflict has always attracted a great deal of interest. It is because of this, trade conflict between the US and China, the geo-political conflict between India and Pakistan will continue to make front-page news.

Crime: This topic has always made news. In case the crime committed is associated with the rich and the famous, it is a page-one story. Newspapers have an exclusive crime reporter for covering such incidents. The crime reporters keep themselves posted about the latest developments and maintain regular contact with police and other investigative agencies. The murder of *The Indian Express* correspondent Shivani Bhatnagar and the arrest of a senior IPS officer continued to hog the limelight for long. The death of Sunanda Pushkar at a posh Delhi hotel and subsequent investigations into her husband Shashi Tharoor's role is another example of people's interest in crime stories.

Money: Stories about wealth and poverty have always made fascinating reading. Readers are naturally interested in improving their economic condition. They are also interested in the success stories of the rich and famous. Features and news items about prominent businessmen and industrialists have always been quite popular. After the liberalization of the Indian economy in the nineties, news about young and new billionaires is regularly reported. Indian and global business magazines annually bring out rich-lists of people with the most wealth.

Size: The size of the event or scale of the audience response–how much, how many, how big, how fast. Everything else being equal, a billion is bigger news than a million. A plane crash that kills 180 people is bigger news as compared to a crash without any casualties. Similarly, natural disasters that devastate large geographies or kill thousands of people make for global headlines.

Significance: In case the event promises or threatens to change the course of history, such an event will be covered with great interest. The terror attack on the Indian Parliament in December 2001 and Prime Minister Atal Bihari Vajpayee's bus ride to Pakistan on a peace mission were important watershed events, which evoked news interest from global media.

Other notable events that happened were the Commonwealth Games that India hosted for the first time in 2010. The games were followed closely in India and abroad by sports lovers not just for their love of sport but also for the negative publicity that India generated due to delays, corruption and the collapse of a bridge.

Similarly, India which is known as the world's largest democracy, always has its parliamentary elections keenly followed across the world. Both, the 2014 and the 2019 elections were watched with great interest across the world in which the BJP won the parliamentary majority for the first time ever, making Narendra Modi an undisputed international leader.

The personality and actions of former US President Donald Trump have been subjects of extensive coverage. In the UK, the Brexit issue has taken centre-stage for a long time to the exclusion of other significant issues affecting the social fabric of the ordinary citizen.

Human Interest: Stories based on the human condition, also called human interest, have always been of interest to the readers. The miserable conditions of farmers, status of women in a rapidly changing society, urban unemployed youth, problems of illiteracy, starvation and poor housing conditions come under human interest. Such stories attract the attention of the government, policy makers and the society at large.

The popularity of social media in the past few years has changed the way media organisations now report human interest or personal stories. With an increasing number of young people getting news updates from social media, there is more focus on personal stories, especially of people bringing about positive change in their communities. Often these stories go viral as people like to share an uplifting story.

Celebrities: They have always been a subject of public attention and, therefore, media coverage. Stories about sports stars, film stars, models, television actors, business tycoons, political leaders and religious leaders are always reported prominently. A more recent addition to this list is 'influencers'—people who have such a wide following on social media that they have become celebrities.

The P3P (Page 3 People) section that comprises socialites, party-hoppers, models and designers, the rich and fashionable fall into this category. The city pages of the newspapers are full of stories about their day-to-day lives, professional activities and personal affairs. This trend has emerged as a part of films, fashion, food and lifestyle journalism.

Self-interest: A reader naturally asks: what is in it for me? How will it affect my life, my job, my family, my community? Therefore, for him the latest news about taxes on personal income and increase in the prices of petrol and other consumer goods is more important than the budget deficit at the national level.

Sources of News

Every reporter develops and nurtures sources of information and news. Most of these sources emanate from their beats and assignments, others are cultivated during the course of professional duties and through personal and social contacts. Some of the important sources of news are:

The Government: The government, consisting of political leaders as well as the bureaucracy, constitutes one of the biggest sources of news simply because it takes decisions which impact almost everyone in the country. It includes the government at the central level as well as the governments of states and union territories.

Ministers and senior officials announce new decisions, hold news conferences and issue press releases from time to time. Some of the important not-to-be-missed government events which are compulsory for the media are the President's Address to the Parliament, presentation of the annual budget and rail budget before the Parliament and similar other policy announcements.

Apart from these formal events and occasions, reporters also get a lot of their news through informal contacts.

Political Parties: Both the ruling and the opposition parties are a big source of news. All media organisations have senior reporters assigned to political parties from where they dig out information related to the policies and programmes of the ruling party. The reporters seek the opinion of the opposition leaders as well as the critique of the government from the opposition parties. Considerable gossip and speculation regularly emanate from the political parties.

In India, political reporting at the national level has always been considered an important responsibility. Senior journalists who cover political parties have easy access to the government. They have sources, cultivated over a period of time, who help them build a perspective beyond the stated public positions of the political parties. All political parties have established media departments and senior leaders are appointed as spokespersons who hold press conferences and briefings regularly.

Civil Society Organisations: Civil Society Organisations constituting NGOs, research institutes, trade unions and professional bodies play a significant role in contemporary society. Many work in important areas, have influence, hold conferences, publish findings and conduct research on varied socio-political changes. Such organisations espouse popular causes—upholding of human rights, environmental protection, women empowerment, education as a fundamental right, and several others. This gives media an opportunity to practice serious journalism with a social purpose. CSOs are a big source of news, information, reports and data for journalists. These organisations provide many news stories to the media related to corruption, inefficiency or malpractices of the government. Many such organisations release research that is new and influences the policies of the government.

Industry Bodies: In this age of globalisation, business and commercial organisations have been playing an important consultative role in shaping and formulating business and economic policies. These bodies regularly interact with the media and whenever an economic issue comes up, journalists contact these organisations for seeking their opinion. Several national-level business organisations—Confederation of Indian Industry (CII), Federation of Indian Chambers of Commerce and Industry (FICCI) and Associated Chambers of Commerce and Industry (ASSOCHAM)—play a leading role in helping shape the economic policies of the country. They organise seminars, hold conferences and provide a forum to political leaders and captains of industry to spell out their views on business and economic issues.

Hospitals: They are an important source of information about health issues, disease, accidents and death. All the concerned reporters maintain regular contact with hospital administrations and with their key contacts in the medial fraternity. These are important sources of news because hospitals have unions and associations of *karamcharis*, nurses, resident doctors as well as senior staff members who provide information to reporters.

Specialists and Experts: It is important for a news organisation to have lists of specialists and experts in various fields who can be contacted for an opinion or a quote on a new development. They are important sources of information for referencing because often a reporter needs advice and explanation related to specialized topics and has to reach out to subject-matter experts for clarity.

Experts and specialists are people with exceptional knowledge and in-depth information on issues such as health and disease, environment and urban affairs, law and crime, constitution and politics, defence and foreign affairs etc. These include people who are researchers, retired government officials, former ambassadors, professionals working in academic institutions and NGOs etc.

Educational Institutions: The education reporter generates news and information from schools, colleges and universities. The sources of information are students, teachers and professors and various bodies, such as student and teacher associations. The information ranges from routine updates, such as the admission process, cut-off lists for various courses, student body elections to off-beat news, such as information relating to new courses, research and innovation and excellence in academics.

Police and Investigative Agencies: The police department, traffic police, fire brigade, investigative agencies, such as the Central Bureau of Investigation (CBI), Criminal Investigation Department (CID) are a vital source of crime news.

With rise in financial, white-collared and cyber crime, new kinds of investigative agencies are being set up. These include agencies which can investigate crime related to business and financial frauds, cyber crimes like phishing, online crimes like stealing the identity of people and harassment over social media. A lot of these crimes pertain to new modes of investigation and the police has to rely on technology for investigation.

Courts: India has a three-tier system of administering justice—the Supreme Court, various high courts and the district courts—that look at thousands of cases everyday. Besides these, the government has provided for the consumer courts in every district to resolve disputes that relate to buyer-seller discontent. Every newspaper has a number of reporters who cover these courts on a daily basis. Some of the most interesting news stories come from the courtrooms and through the judgements and observations of the courts.

It is not just disputes between individuals that make news, but also the pronouncements by courts on the functioning of the government, the police and civic agencies. Another important source of news from the courtrooms are the Public Interest Litigations (PILs) filed by individuals and NGOs.

News Values

Accuracy: The most important attribute of journalism is to report facts accurately and build credibility. Therefore, the media has to take care not to present inaccurate, misleading or distorted statements. While writing a news report, a reporter must check names, facts and figures. A reporter may have to go back to the source to ensure that the information is correct and factual. The editor who is editing and rewriting the story also has to keep a sharp eye to ensure that spellings, grammar and facts are accurate. Mistakes leads to loss of credibility besides legal and professional problems for the reporter and the news organisation.

Objectivity: The news report has to be objective—which means that both sides and all points of view are fairly presented. Carrying only one version and ignoring others in the coverage of a news item amounts to taking sides. A reporter should avoid reference to points about which they are not sure. If such a point has to be introduced, the story should clarify that it has not been confirmed. A reporter should take care not to mix personal opinion in a news story and should report on facts without taking sides. A good journalist will not allow personal, political, ideological, regional or religious biases to influence his reporting.

Clarity: Clarity and precision are important attributes of a news story. It is important that a story is written in a manner that it can be easily understood by readers. This can be achieved only through consistent writing practice and mastery over the language. Excessive data and wordiness tend to confuse readers. It is, therefore, essential that a reporter should use short sentences and paragraphs. Complicated and long sentences make it difficult for a reader to understand the story properly.

News People Want

All human beings want a healthier and happier life for themselves and their families. They also, perhaps unconsciously, expect the media to help them with information that goes beyond news and is useful to them in various ways. Readers, therefore, do not just want hardcore news but also features, interviews and opinions that will inform them about the following:

- *Ways to improve their economic and political situation*: Informative stories about business developments, employment opportunities and positions, career development, educational opportunities, managing family budgets, generating income through various financial instruments, preparing for retirement and other such aspects which make living easier and comfortable.
- *Improvement or deterioration in the quality of living:* Quality of air and water, in short, the immediate environment affecting daily lives, city crime which affects security, vanishing wildlife, housing and similar aspects which have a bearing on the daily lives of people.
- *Conditions of individual freedom:* Infringement and violation of human rights, censorship on dissemination of news and restrictions on movement of individuals within their state or the country.
- *Ways to extend and enjoy life:* Medical discovery, improvement in healthcare facilities, information about fitness and holistic wellbeing.
- *Gadgets and technology:* With innovations and rapid changes taking place in information technology and gadgetry like mobile phones, music devices and laptops, people want to be ahead of their peer group in understanding and using technology.

Structure of News: Inverted Pyramid Style

The news story is written in the inverted pyramid style with the most significant fact at the top. The other facts follow in their order of importance except in special circumstances. This enables a story to remain self-contained, no matter how much of it is deleted at the end. For this reason, the first part of the story must bring out the dramatic importance of the event.

Schools of journalism talk about a news story being composed like an inverted pyramid. This means if you turn the pyramid on its head you have the broad base at the top. The broad base of a well-written story consists of the intro, followed by the rest of the story in a mixture of chronological order and importance so that the last sentences or paragraphs of the story are of the least importance. Even though the inverted pyramid style has developed in journalism over the years, it follows the traditional story structure.

There are two advantages in presenting the story in the inverted style. First, if the reader does not read till the end, and a number of readers do that, they still have the essential facts. From the production point of view, it is much easier for the sub-editor to cut down the story from the bottom, rather than edit a word here or there to reduce its length.

The inverted pyramid format assists:

- The reporter, who uses it to compose facts quickly,
- The editor, who can delete the last few paragraphs of a story to make it fit the page, and
- The reader who can tell at a glance if he is interested in the story.

This format has been criticised as being old fashioned and traditional. However, the inverted pyramid has survived and will probably do so in the future as well.

Elements of the New Story—5Ws and 1H

Traditionally, the general format for a well-written newspaper story is that it tells who did what, where, when, and why. These "five Ws" constitute essential features of any good story along with one "H" which stands for How.

In this context, Rudyard Kipling's rhyme outlines the entire nature of news writing:

> *"I keep six honest serving men*
> *they taught me all I knew:*
> *Their names are,*
> *What and Why and When*
> *And How and Where and Who."*

We will discuss this aspect of news structuring in detail in the chapter on reporting.

News as an Event and a Process: In its report on the Future of Print Media, the Press Council of India suggested in 2001 that in the context of developing countries, the concept of news needed to be expanded. The report says: In developing countries, the concept of news appears to need expansion to take in not only the 'event' but the entire 'process'. For instance, hunger is a process while a hunger strike is an event; a flood is an event, a struggle to control floods or deforestation is a process.

Hard News: Hard news stories make up a major part of news reporting. These stories generally embody the 4Ws and 1H as discussed above. Hard news consists of basic facts: who, what, when, where and how. It is the news of important public events, accidents, happenings and announcements. These will consist of government announcements, international events, crime and other spot news items. The front pages of newspapers and the lead stories on television channels and radio stations usually comprise hard news. These news items are perishable, which must be reported to the public in a timely manner. These cannot be delayed at all.

Stories of disaster, crime and war, major political developments—all constitute hard news. The bigger the personality, the bigger the story. Something that affects a thousand people makes stronger news than something which affects ten.

Soft News: It focuses on situations, people or events that have human interest. Such stories are generally not sharply focused in time and can often be held back. Soft news generally discusses issues that are topical and in the news. Human interest stories and features come under the soft news category.

Backgrounder: In the event of a major news story that has wide ramifications, the reporters along with the help of the editors will prepare detailed background reports with news, feature articles, quotes from important people, historical perspective and infographics. Also called depth reports, these help a reader get a wider perspective to the main news story. Background material gives readers explanation, traces the development of the event and adds facts which may not have been available in the original story. This type of writing is explanatory, arising from the analytical coverage of social, economic or educational issues.

Newspapers have taken to using backgrounders frequently to keep their readers fully informed about all aspects of news. All news agencies regularly provide background features on subjects like health, technology, science, agriculture and environment.

News Analysis: Newspapers have been resorting to magazine-style journalism—the genre of writing called news analysis that serves the readers with analysis and interpretation of events. While hard news highlights important aspects of an event, news analysis explores dimensions, which cannot be covered by the news story. With rising competition from the digital media and TV channels, newspapers are increasingly relying on well-researched and well-written analysis. It is in this context that the importance of news analysis needs to be appreciated. Some of the important examples of news analysis are:

An analysis, 'The Balakot strike proves that IAF has come of age' by Shishir Gupta in the *Hindustan Times* says: "The Balakot strike and the riposte to the PAF (Pakistan Air Force) counter on February 27 shows that the IAF has come of age and can no longer be seen as just a force supporting a land offensive. Time and again, the IAF leadership has come out in the open saying that it is a strategic force but till Balakot, perhaps neither the sister forces nor the poitical leadership were too sure.

"...With the Balakot air strike, the IAF has moved to another level of capabilities with the force not afraid to get blooded in battle. While all three services need to synergise their roles in the worst-case scenario, Wing Commander Abhinandan, by downing a superior F-16 fighter with an upgraded MiG-21, showed that the IAF takes the battle to its enemy."

(https://www.hindustantimes.com/analysis/the-balakot-strike-proves-that-iaf-has-come-of-age/story-YvteejkQhEZAvuk1XVgseI.html)

An opinion piece by author Himanshu on June 4, 2019 on the BJP's victory in the parliamentary elections says: "The results of general elections to the 17th Lok Sabha have given the incumbent Bharatiya Janata Party (BJP) another full majority after the 2014 verdict. While most people expected the BJP to come back to power, the margin of victory in many seats has surprised many. However, these elections were not only about electing a new government. The verdict of the electorate delivered on 23 May, 2019 has lessons for the BJP as well as for the opposition. While it is difficult to analyse various factors that contributed to the victory of the BJP, one of the major factors will remain the personal credibility of Prime Minister Narendra Modi. The opposition certainly lacks a credible face that can take on Modi. The fact that the BJP successfully played out the narrative of national security is also beyond doubt.

However, the election results are also puzzling, given the track record of the BJP in assembly elections. After May 2014, in all the assembly elections held until May 2019, the BJP was successful in winning states ruled by opposition parties but failed to retain BJP-ruled states, except Gujarat and Goa. In both these states where it managed to retain its state governments, it formed a government with a reduced majority. Clearly, at the state level, the BJP is far more successful in dislodging opposition governments than retaining power. However, in the Lok Sabha, it has not only won as an incumbent, but has also managed to increase its vote share and number of seats."

(https://www.livemint.com/opinion/columns/opinion-why-modi-remains-the-preferred-choice-of-the-electorate-1559586663012.html)

The above examples provide an insight or an explanation to readers which do not form a part of the breaking news story. Such articles help readers comprehend news better. The news analysis is, therefore, an important genre of contemporary journalism.

REFERENCES

James M. Neal and Suzanne S. Brown (2000). *Newswriting and Reporting*, The Iowa State University Press.

Melvin L. DeFleur and Everette E. Dennis (1994). *Understanding Mass Communication*, Houghton Mifflin Company.

Melvin Mencher (1999). *Basic News Writing*, Universal Book Stall, New Delhi.

3

News Organisation

Newspapers and News Agencies

Newspapers and news agencies are considered the heartbeat of media systems of a country. They are the major purveyors of news and information to the people.

The growing demand for news and rise in literacy has led to a phenomenal increase in the readership and daily circulation of newspapers which reach tens of millions of readers. Newspapers continue to shape opinions in the 'global village' of today. Satellites are being used for long distance transmission of journalistic information. The advances in information technology and communication have brought a great increase in the speed and timeliness of journalistic activity. At the same time the new technologies have provided massive outlets and audiences for the electronically distributed products. The cost of large-scale news gathering led to the formation of news agencies and organisations that sell their national and international news to many different individual newspapers and magazines.

The companion volume of this book, *Handbook of Journalism and Mass Communication*, has discussed in detail salient features of leading newspapers and news agencies in the section on *Print Media*. The section on *Media Management* discusses organizational structure of the editorial department and newsroom organisation of a daily newspaper. Here we shall discuss several other aspects of the working of these organisations.

Newspapers

Let us view the perception of a senior journalist, Gulab Kothari about a newspaper who, in his book *Newspaper Management in India*, says: "A newspaper plays a crucial role in society. Besides providing information to its readers, a newspaper aims at educating and leading the public at large, and protecting rights and freedom of the people. Giving right perspective to the facts, providing a forum of debate and discussion, inspiring people for cooperation, love and unity, improving quality of life and entertainment are some of its other goals. A newspaper is, therefore, an instrument of social change. It must uphold moral and ethical values in society and provide a truthful, comprehensive and intelligent account of events and give meaning to them. Undoubtedly, a newspaper must act with responsibility, be fair and independent and neutral and objective".

These are the ideals that Kothari wishes a newspaper to adapt and emulate. It is a different matter that some proprietors consider the newspaper as a product which is produced like any other industrial product. This 'product' must be financially viable, should be able to succeed in the face of market conditions and reflect the trends of the society, rather than educating and leading public at large, as is enunciated by Kothari.

Let us examine the editorial working of a newspaper because it is the editorial guidance and leadership that give a newspaper its personality and importance. Here we shall confine ourselves to the editorial working of the newspaper and not several other, equally important, sections like advertising, circulation and printing.

Editorial Management

Although newspapers throughout the world differ widely in range, size, subjects and interests covered by them, all papers have two basic divisions: the business and editorial operations. The business side generally manages the financial affairs, marketing and circulation; whereas the editorial side includes reporters, sub-editors and all others who gather news and process information to convert it into news, thus, making the paper what it is.

The editorial staff comprises people who produce the news contents of the paper—gather, write and edit stories, handle photographs, design and produce infographics and prepare the final selection of news for printing. Heading the entire team is the editor. In some newspapers he is titled as editor-in-chief or executive editor.

Editor

The editor holds the key post in the newspaper organisation. He is the head of the editorial department. The editor has to develop a presentation style of the newspaper that is attractive and highly reader-friendly, besides, he has to ensure consistency of style throughout the paper. Baskette and Sissors have succinctly remarked that the editor is a diamond cutter who refines and polishes, removes the flaws and shapes a stone into a gem. He searches for ills in copy and meticulously scans the product for flaws and inaccuracy, ever searching for the maximum power of words.

The editor works directly for the publisher and is responsible for the paper's contents, with the exception of advertising. He is responsible for formulating editorial policies of the newspaper. He is also responsible for Team Building—he appoints reporters, feature writers and reviewers and ensures that all persons working in the editorial department work as a team. He provides leadership to the editorial team.

In the past, there were editors who wrote only editorials, or articles on specialised subjects. They were the writer-editors and believed in the privacy of the editorial page. However, the situation is fast changing. Eminent editor and author T.J.S. George, in his book Editing—A Handbook for Journalists, says about the future editor: "The editor will have to be a generalist knowing something about everything, leading a team of specialists who know everything about something. Specialization must come into its own—not only specialist writers/ reporters on a variety of subjects but also specialists in re-writing, subbing, research, design and typography. If depth and range are what will help the print media hold its own against electronic competition, this kind of re-orientation will be unavoidable for our newspapers itching for a revaluation".

The functions of an editor have transcended editorial duties. His control is now merged into the managerial side of the paper under which he may exercise both a journalistic and commercial influence. A Press Council of India (PCI) report, *Future of Print Media*, highlights the changing role and importance of the office of the editor: "Unfortunately the developments in the press in the last few decades have done a great disservice to the institution of the editor. The primary cause of the devaluation of the office of the editor is not that newspapers are run as a business not only because they earn profit but also because they wield enormous power. What is more, they are not ordinarily accountable for their day-do-day conduct to any authority.... Commercialisation of the press and the devaluation of the office of the editor have gone to such a length that instead of the editor, we have now the Managing Editor who manages both the economies and the contents of the newspapers; the Resident Editor who is controlled from above by the management and now the Brand Manager who is supposed to effect coordination between the different departments of the newspaper establishment according to the respondent newspaper...."

News Editor

The most important ingredient of any newspaper is the news. Therefore, it stands to reason that we cannot have a good newspaper if we do not have a good news editor. The news editor is the fountainhead and provides leadership to the newsroom. News is not merely what happens; it is also what can be made to happen.

A news editor heads the News Desk and is the sole in-charge of the diary. He is constantly looking at it to ensure that all items listed in the date are properly covered in the newspaper. In the news diary he lists all the up-coming events and alerts his editor. The news editor has to deal with selection and placement of news. As he is responsible for all the news stories that appear in a newspaper, he is an experienced and senior journalist of long standing with a nose for news.

It is the duty of news editor to build up the news service of the newspaper on a sound footing. He has to keep in touch with his newspaper's other editorial heads—the Metro Editor, the Business Editor, the Sports Editor as well as the numerous state correspondents, even the foreign reporters on an hourly basis. He has to keep checking with them about the important news that is happening on their beats and also to alert them and other colleagues about news developments happening elsewhere. His other job is to keep an eye on national and international news agencies for the latest happenings.

A good news editor is always thinking of today's news besides stories that are likely to happen in the near future. For instance, if the budget is due in a week's time, he has to plan the likely stories, provide news ideas to correspondents, asks reporters to interview a cross-section of people on what to expect from the budget.

The News Editor also plans the selection of news and the placement of news within the newspaper—whether a particular news should be taken on page one or on the inside pages. If the news has to be taken on page one, he also decides the placement of the item—whether it is the top story of the day, a story of lesser importance or should be placed at the bottom of page one. He is the one who decides the number of columns to be allotted to the story and whether it should have a photograph or not. Depending on the importance of the news item, he also checks with the respective heads of the departments if an analytical article or a backgrounder is coming along with the news item.

In all these duties related to the selection, handling, design and placement of news, the News Editor is helped by the Chief Sub-editor and many Sub-editors.

Chief Sub-editor

Late S. Prakasa Rao, Director of the Press Institute of India (PII) observed: "The primary responsibility of the Chief Sub-editor is to scan all the wordage, digest the mass of copy, reject or accept, select or omit and give the best to the reader. The Chief Sub-editor produces the edition. He makes the world come alive in the stories, in the headlines and in the make-up of the newspaper. This means that the Chief Sub-editor must have imagination, understanding, sympathy, a knowledge of political affairs and insight."

The Chief-Sub, as he is popularly called, must know his city, his state, his country, the people, their leaders and their problems. He must know the working of the civic bodies, the legislature and the courts. The Chief-Sub must have some knowledge of sports and commerce as well as international situation, interests of the super powers and problems of the Third World. He must understand the significance of events and should have a good news sense.

While distributing the copy to his team of Sub-editors, the Chief-Sub instructs them on the length of the reports and the site and type of headlines he would like and decide also the place for them in the paper. Sometimes the Chief-Sub may himself edit important stories. It is his duty to ascertain facts which are missing and checks these from the Reporters.

Sub-editor

A number of Sub-editors form part of the team under the Chief Sub-editor. The Sub-editor's daily task is to keep track of news agencies, select news that is worthy of being taken for the day, make layout of the page, edit the copy, give headlines and finally fill up the page with news. A Sub-editor's skills include not just news selection, but editing as well as the knowledge of various software used for designing a page.

A newspaper receives news from a number of sources—reporters, correspondents and news agencies. All this information is filtered by the Sub-editor in consultation with the Chief Sub-editor. Often in case of breaking news, there may be a number of developments with a confusing picture. The correspondent may give a different story, whereas the news agencies may give their own account. In such cases, the Sub-editor has to put all the conflicting accounts together and eliminate confusion by checking with the newspaper's own correspondent. It is thus the responsibility of the Sub-editor to make the story logical. A Sub-editor should see to it that the news is based upon facts, is as complete as possible, and is clear from every angle.

A Sub-editor should have an absolute command over the language, have an eye for accuracy and must look out for errors. In case of missing facts, he should ask these from the reporter. He must keep himself informed about the daily developments of a news story and be prepared for any news that breaks out suddenly.

He should be competent to reduce a lengthy paragraph to its deserving size. He must be capable of reducing the subject matter as per the space and be prepared to pad up a news item with background information if the need arises. He checks the spellings of names and places, correct errors of grammar, capitalization, punctuation and abbreviations. A good Sub-editor has the knack of getting to the heart of the story quickly. Once all of this is done, the Sub-editor also writes a suitable headline for the story.

As every newspaper has a character of its own, one of the essentials to maintain that character is to have uniformity and consistency in the spelling of words and names of people. Whenever necessary, the Sub-editor consults the style book of the newspaper. The satisfaction for a Sub-editor lies in a job well done—satisfaction in improving copy by deleting jargon, complex and difficult words. Writing bright headlines is another important contribution of a Sub-editor.

We have discussed the usage of correct language in various chapters. Here more examples are given: The editorial style book of *The Patriot*, Delhi, contains an interesting example. It says: "Kill sentences like this: With regard to the discussion which took place at yesterday's meeting in reference to the position arising out of the present situation, the result, so far as the practical point of view is concerned, was of a purely negative character."

The Patriot's style book rightly points out 'Nothing came of yesterday's discussions' is enough. Five words instead of forty and a great deal of clarity.

News Agencies

No newspaper, however well staffed, can hope to survive without the help of news agencies. News agencies bring in a constant flow of well-edited news from all over the world. This helps a newspaper plug in news gaps from areas where it is not represented through its reporters or stringers. On the other hand news agencies are active and ticking round the clock.

Since a news agency serves a variety of clientele—newspapers, electronic media networks, individuals and other media establishments with varying ideologies and opinions—it can hardly afford to deviate from the straight path of factual reporting. As a matter of policy, a news agency generally abstains from editorializing, commenting and interpreting.

News agencies are also known as wire services. We know the major international news agencies that dominate the world are: AFP (Agence France Presse), AP (Associated Press) and Reuters. Each of these wire services has offices or bureaus throughout the world. Their services are utilized by magezines, newspapers, major TV networks and radio stations all over the world. The dependence of newspapers on wire services is underlined by the fact that news agencies bring them not only national and international news, but also cartoons, comic strips, crosswords, puzzles and news features. There are a number of agencies exclusively providing photographs as well.

AP's Prescription for Lead: News agencies, right from the beginning, changed the very concept of how the news was being reported in the newspapers. In this context the comments in *Understanding Mass Communication* are noteworthy: "In the early days, sending stories by telegraph was very expensive and clarity and precision were essential. The correspondent in the field had less time for the flowery language and elongated sentences common to early nineteenth century newspapers." Before long, reporters and editors began to distinguish between 'telegraph' and 'newspaper' stories. The concise writing needed for wire services eventually produced AP's famous prescription for a lead: "who, what, where, when and why." Stories transmitted by wire were organised in the inverted pyramid style, in which the most important elements were first, the next important second, and so on. Thus, if a local newspaper needed to save space, a story could easily be shortened by dropping less important details from the tail of the pyramid."

News Agency Style

Most of the news agencies have developed their own style which has been codified in the form of a Style Book. The Non-Aligned News Agencies Pool (NANAP) brought out a Style Book based on principles which are of universal relevance in news collection, processing and dissemination. Some of the salient points forming the style book are summarized below:

Lead of a News Story: The opening paragraph or lead of a news story should be short and crisp, so as to catch attention and direct the reader's interest to the body of the story. It should not be cluttered with details that can wait until later in the copy. If a reader has to look over a sentence a second time to understand it, then that sentence has no place in news agency copy. It certainly will not make the lead. A news story must answer the three Ws: What? When? and Where? As a rule the answers to these should find place in the opening paragraph.

Simplicity: A news copy should be written in simple and familiar language understood by the average reader. Simple, direct sentences are more effective than long, winding ones. A simple style enables all levels of the population, the rustic villager as much as the urban elite, to grasp the contents of a news item. Further, where news reports require to be translated, especially for multi-language societies as in India, it makes the task of translation easier and speedier. Unfamiliar words and jargon (expressions peculiar to fields of special knowledge) should be avoided as far as possible. The choice of words should be simple and elegant. When not avoidable, as in a quotation, the unfamiliar words should be explained in simpler language.

Active Voice: The active voice is generally more effective in a news copy. "The Government today announced the appointment of a committee to study and report on..." has a better flow than: "The appointment of a committee to study and report on... was announced by the Government today." Similarly, "India and Yugoslavia today signed an agreement providing for...." reads much better than "an agreement between India and Yugoslavia, providing for... was signed here today."

However, in certain circumstances the passive voice is useful, especially where the deed is more important than the doer. Thus, "A general strike has been called for tomorrow by… to protest against..." is more pointed than "The… has called a general strike for tomorrow in protest against...".

Identification: All persons named in a copy should be properly identified. Where the subject of a copy has multiple identifications, that is if he or she can be identified in more ways than one, the most pertinent among them—as a rule the office or position of consequence he or she currently holds—should be mentioned in the first instance, the others being suitably mentioned in later parts of the copy. Where the subject does not hold any office currently, he or she should be identified by the former office.

Objectivity and the Use of Proper Language: Carrying only one version and ignoring others in the coverage of a controversial matter amounts to taking sides. Objectivity demands that both sides or all the points of view in a controversy are fairly presented.

A journalist should avoid reference to points about which he himself is not sure. If such a point has to be introduced, the copy should clarify that it is unconfirmed. Similarly, in view of the requirement of strict objectivity, no adjective or any other expression that smacks of bias, involves a value judgment or any snide or sarcastic observations, can be allowed in a news agency copy. An exception is when such an expression is part of a quotation, and that too, if it is material to the story and has no defamatory implication.

Similarly, an agency can neither justify nor criticize any action by anyone, whether in authority or otherwise, since that constitutes a value judgment. For instance, it is not permissible to say, "The police had to open fire..." or "… was forced to open fire." The correct way is to say, "The police opened fire," which is a factual narration. However, if an official or a political leader states that the police had to open fire, that may be attributed to them.

Sourcing: A news agency has to be particular about its source of news. There are certain types of stories where no source is required, for instance, proceedings of legislatures and courts, or meetings and conferences. In all other cases, a news agency report requires to be authenticated with a proper source, since the agency itself does not accept any responsibility for the statement issued or facts offered by any person. By dropping mention of the source, the agency would be needlessly accepting responsibility for views in information which may be open to question.

The Editor and General Manager of the UNI, late G.G. Mirchandani, offered the following tips to the newsroom staff on reporting accidents, communal incidents and crime.

Accidents: Report with utmost caution the accidents involving defence establishments. Quote a competent authority. In other cases, quote a police, railway or district official or head of the establishment or service. Mention the time and place of the occurrence and give the announced cause of the accident. In describing an accident, show respect to the dead. Avoid gory details, and do not give the names of those killed unless announced authoritatively. Legal complications may arise if you kill a person who is alive.

Describe accurately the nature of the accident, whether it was a crash, collision, sinking, house collapse, derailment, capsizing, skidding off, belly-landing, cloud burst or landslide. Do not give your own assessment of the damage, loss or suffering caused by an accident. All such informations should be attributed to competent persons. Be objective. Do not exaggerate.

Communal Incidents: Greatest care should be exercised in reporting communal clashes. Do not identify communities revolved in a clash, nor should you refer to them as the majority or minority community. Generalised allegations and accusations of being anti-social or anti-national should not be made against an individual or a community. Do not give any facts or figures without verification. If their publication is likely to arouse communal passions, they should not be reported. The source from which estimates of damage or casualty figures are obtained must be indicated. If unconfirmed figures must be filed because confirmed figures are unavailable or not forthcoming, indicate that your figures are unconfirmed, or are from a non-official source which must be identified.

News of incidents involving loss of life, lawlessness and arson should be reported strictly in an objective manner and attributed to a competent authority. Do not say a temple, mosque or church was set afire. Refer to it as a place of worship. Similarly, use the term holy book for the *Gita*, the *Koran* or the *Bible*.

Crime: In reporting crimes such as murder, suicide, arson, sabotage and the like, information regarding the persons involved, the motive or cause should be attributed to a source. Do not say a person was arrested unless confirmed by the police. A person may be detained, held for questioning or may cooperate with an investigation without having been formally arrested. While reporting the arrest of an individual, give the charge against him. In the eyes of the law a person is presumed to be innocent until he is found guilty by a court. Therefore, avoid describing a suspect or an accused as a culprit (which implies guilt). Instead, call him an alleged assailant or alleged spy. Do not give names of minors involved in crime. Attribute to the police all information provided by them. Refrain from making conjectures about the manner in which a crime was committed, nor should you comment, draw conclusions or support or discount a particular theory.

These guidelines from the veteran journalist, who spent a lifetime in the service of the profession, are equally valid for all reporters. These salient points have been extracted and summarised from the style book of the NANAP, 1985.

Feature Syndicates

Besides news agencies, a number of feature syndicates have been providing news features to news organisations. Earlier, these syndicates would deliver news material, cartographic services and pictures by hand or mail. With change in technologies, they began to provide their services through the internet or by logging into their websites. Some of these agencies are INFA (Indian News and Features Alliance), Inter Press Service (IPS), Panos and Women's Features Service (WFS). Over the last few years Panos and WFS have closed down. In USA, these syndicates provide a remarkable variety of entertainment and opinion material for newspapers including columns by political commentators, serialization of popular books, comic strips, movie reviews and columns on astrology, books, and politics.

Over the last many years, a number of media organisations have started their own syndicated services offering articles to other publications for a fee or under an arrangement. Several Indian newspapers have been making use of such services provided by newspapers such as *The New York Times, The Guardian, The Observer* and *The Telegraph*. Such arrangements by news organisations meet the requirement of newspapers seeking diversity of news and write-ups on specialist subjects. In recent years, sports writing and analysis has seen a big jump in syndicated writing by eminent sportspersons and commentators.

Khushwant Singh and Kuldeep Nayyar, both well-known writers, had a large fan followings of their syndicated columns. Their columns are translated into several languages and published by newspapers across the country. Nayyar had this useful advice for young journalists:

"They should stay in regular jobs to earn experience and reputation. For a syndicated columnist, it is important that he has a name and that his credibility is established."

NOTES

1. *Future of Print Media (2001), Press Council of India.*
2. Floud K. Baskette and Zack Z. Sissors (1971): *The Art of Editing*, Macmillan Publishing Company, New York.

REFERENCES

Gulab Kothari (1995): *Newspaper Management in India*, Inter-cultural Open University, The Netherlands.

Indian Institute of Mass Communication (1978): *A Manual for News Agency Reporters*, New Delhi.

Melvin L. DeFleur and Everette E. Dennis (1994): *Understanding Mass Communication*, Houghton Mifflin Company, Boston.

Kamath, M.V. (1980): *Professional Journalism*, Vikas Publishing House Pvt. Ltd., New Delhi.

4

Magazine Journalism

The Phenomenon of Niche Magazines

The evolution of Indian readership over the past 20 years makes for a fascinating study. With higher levels of income and educational levels, and increasing awareness about news and current affairs, the readers are no longer satisfied with what newspapers have to offer. The Indian reader today has become demanding and is willing to pay the price of a newspaper or magazine that meets his needs, besides affording time for news on television. Indian news magazines have shown that, in addition to the inevitable political diet, there are other aspects of life that are of interest: the arts, science, films and fashion, travel and sports, leisure and lifestyle. These aspects need an altogether different treatment and approach.

Even as the younger audiences move to smart phones and social media platforms for their news and information needs, many readers retain interest in magazines of various kinds.

Evolution of Magazines

One of the reasons for the magazine boom in the country is that magazines set about giving readers a better-packaged product in terms of well-written stories with a strong visual appeal. Magazines discovered the unfulfilled needs of newspaper readers in a dramatically emerging middle class. This required the employment of designers and well-paid editorial staff of a high calibre, coupled with willingness to spend time and money on well-researched stories. News magazines appeared as if on the dot to cater to the changing needs of the reader.

Magazine journalism is a different ball game as compared to writing for the online media or for newspapers. It falls neither in the category of daily reporting as is the case with newspapers, nor is it as fast-paced as is the case with digital journalism or television reporting. However, with the advent of the digital media and the strong influence of social media websites, magazine journalism has changed swiftly—both in the way it provides news and also in its nature. All the mainstream magazine publishers, like *India Today*, *Outlook* and others have now launched a number of niche magazines to retain their hold over advertising and also over their readers. Owing to the changing dynamics—an open economy and competition from various quarters, mainstream magazines have morphed over a period of time. Magazines like *India Today* which were monthly news magazines decades back have evolved into weekly magazines while others like *The Illustrated Weekly of India* folded up. Similarly, *Time Magazine* of the US reduced its print considerably to focus on the online edition.

The magazines give readers less immediate news and more analysis, detailed articles, features and backgrounders. A number of times during a year, magazines may bring out well-researched articles on social trends, health, lifestyle and education to provide in-depth and data-based information for their readers. Taking a cue from magazines, newspapers have introduced weekly feature pages on topics environment, gadgets, living and similar other subjects. The magazine sections of newspapers, have seen tremendous success as newspapers copied the attractive designs and trendy stories published in magazines.

With many media houses venturing into holding events, conclaves and summits, magazines now carry detailed information from such events also. These summits address contemporary affairs—politics, sports, technology, foreign affairs, and invite top thought leaders and renowned politicians from across the world. Sometimes, an entire issue of a magazine may be devoted to the event that the magazine has organised. The India Today Group organises the India Today Conclave besides other events while Femina organises the Miss World beauty contest.

News Magazines

Today, hundreds of high-quality magazines exist in India, published in several languages. *India Today* was first launched in 1975 in English and gradually expanded into Hindi, Tamil, Malayalam and Telugu editions. From a single magazine, the India Today Group spans television channels, the daily newspaper *Mail Today* and has numerous tie-ups with foreign publications to market their editions in India.[1] The magazine achieved breakthrough after the Emergency ended in 1977 as it caught the attention of the readers through its well-researched articles published by young, enthusiastic and hardworking journalists.

The magazine boom could not have occurred without the improvements in printing technology, and the support of commercial advertising, where colour advertisements greatly enhanced the attractiveness of magazines. The Indian media scene is bustling with news magazines of various kinds. It was in 1995 when a construction company decided to launch the weekly magazine *Outlook* that gave *India Today* a tough competition. Very soon, the magazine broke some sensational stories and made a permanent mark on the Indian news scene. A few years later, it launched other publications notably *Outlook Traveller* and *Outlook* in Hindi.[2]

Another magazine, the *Caravan* was relaunched in 2010 as a monthly magazine which calls itself, "India's first long-form narrative journalism magazine." Soon after its relaunch, it garnered considerable attention for its detailed, investigative and research-based reporting, often upsetting powerful people who rushed to file court cases against it. Many of its journalists have received prestigious journalism awards.

It is not just the weekly magazines, even fortnightly magazines have maintained their hold on the Indian reader. Take the example of *Frontline*, brought out by The Hindu group of publications.[3] First published in 1984, *Frontline* is known for its in-depth reporting and takes pride in keeping the spotlight on social, environmental and science-related issues.

Another magazine to be brought out from South India is *The Week*, first published in 1982 by the Malayala Manorama group. It is one of the largest weekly news magazines in India and the group itself is one of the older and bigger entities in the Indian media. The Malayala Manorama group brings out publications in five languages and has a considerable digital presence. Besides reaching out to readers in India, it also caters to ethnic Indians in various countries.

One of the latest weekly news magazines, *Open* was launched in 2009 from 12 cities simultaneously. Close to its competitors in terms of news, analysis and reporting, it also has carved out a market for itself in a crowded magazine space. The mainstream news magazine market is competitive with *India Today*, *Outlook*, *The Week* and *Open* fighting for the readers' attention. However, magazines like *Frontline*—a fortnightly, and *Caravan*—a monthly, are equally sought after as they have developed a committed readership for themselves.

On the other side are business news magazines which are equally sought after for their news, analysis and views on government policy, corporates, business and economy. The readership for business magazines is completely different as compared to the mainstream magazines. For entrepreneurs, businessmen and executives, it is important to stay informed about the trends in the markets and stay ahead of the competition. Though most of the business magazines are by Indian publishing houses, there are a few foreign publishing houses that have launched their local editions in the country. *Forbes* and *Fortune* are the two foreign magazines that have made an impact in the Indian business news market.

Amongst the business magazines, *Business India* is considered to be the pioneer as it was launched in February 1978—much before the process of liberalisation of the Indian economy began. A fortnightly, it is believed to have laid the ground for other magazines in India. Launched in 1992, *Business Today* from the India Today group became one of the first magazines to write about management theories and provide coverage of the Indian economy in great detail. *Outlook Business* was launched in 1995, soon after the launch of the *Outlook* magazine. It provides detailed analysis of market trends, stock prices and sales strategies. *Business World* is another important business magazine that was founded in 1981 and covers the Indian economy, marketing, advertising and the retail industry.

Business magazines have evolved owing to the opening up of the Indian economy, privatisation, globalisation, the upsurge in digital economy and the emergence of information technology and fin-tech companies. With the intertwining of economies across the world and governments getting deeply involved in economic affairs, the readership of business newspapers and magazines has grown tremendously.

Magazine journalists are usually good writers as they write detailed articles and not merely report the news of the day. They write in-depth features, do analysis and provide more information in their articles to make the reader feel he has received a 360-degree view of the news. Journalists writing for magazines often find themselves under pressure as they are indirectly competing with newspapers and news channels to catch the reader's eye. Therefore, a magazine journalist has to provide more to her reader because the news has already been read, seen and discussed thoroughly. A magazine journalist has to provide an opinion or an analysis in a manner that the reader understands the story behind the news. At the same time, magazines also bring clarity and truth to news—something that is getting lost due to the flourishing and free social media websites where many people from across the society share unverified and uninformed personal opinion. With increasing competition and impact of the digital media and social media websites, publishing houses are bringing out a diversity of magazines that can be termed as niche publications.

Niche Magazines

Over the last two decades, media houses have increasingly ventured into greener pastures of publishing by exploiting the untapped market of niche magazines—lifestyle, travel, food, fashion, gadgets, auto, technology, health, wellness, architecture and many more. One can even write for B2B (business to business) magazines, stocks and trade journals. Check out the stall of any news vendor in the market and you will notice that there are magazines that target everyone in the household—men, women, children, sports lovers and the health freak. Media houses which were publishing only news magazines noticed falling readership due to competition from news channels and later on from the digital media, which was absolutely free. This competition from different sectors of the media made magazine publishers move into different categories of journalism.

This move from news journalism to niche publishing is a global trend and India has not been immune to it. With people getting news instantly on their mobile phones, traditional publishers had to move fast. They expanded their publishing basket beyond the news category. In India, a large number of niche magazines have been launched in collaboration with foreign publications as these publications came from countries where the magazine market was already saturated. Indian media houses innovated and moved into newer segments by tapping into specialised journalism. By launching niche magazines, the media not only developed new readers but also tapped into the information interests of its committed readership with innovative ideas.

It is not just the mainstream media houses that have launched niche magazines. Magazines have been launched even by top car companies, hotels, malls and shopping brands to pamper their buyers, keep them updated about company products and make them feel good about the high-end purchase that they have done. In a consumer oriented market companies feel that bringing out a special monthly magazine that provides shoppers with information regarding the company and its products can make consumers remain loyal to the brand. The in-flight magazines given by airlines, the one-year free subscriptions given to consumers who buy a luxury car, or the ones published by malls or even hotels are examples of such magazines. So, for students of journalism, even brand magazines such as these, which reach out to brand customers, not the general audience, provide good job opportunities.

The increase in the number of niche magazines is also a pointer to the changing economics of the country— the launch of new products, emergence of new brands resulting in the creation of new markets and a new category of consumers. The niche segment satisfies the information needs of consumers who are looking at special kind of reading materials—health, cars, hotels, travel and photography—that cater to their tastes. For the media houses, it has opened up new channels of advertising from companies which would not deem it suitable to advertise in the mainstream media. Niche magazines have allowed these companies to reach out to their desired socio-economic audience for advertising their special, high-end or luxury products. Similarly, hotels and tourism companies may only want to advertise in travel magazines while cosmetics companies may prefer to release their advertisements only in women's magazines.

Writing for the Kerala Press Academy's bilingual monthly journal, *Media*, Shoma A. Chatterji, freelance journalist and author says: "Niche journalism, it may be pointed out, needs expertise both in the niche subject one is writing on as well as the command over journalistic writing. A computer magazine, for instance, will need columnists and journalists who not only know everything they have to know about a particular area of computers, such as virus programmes, but must also have the ability to write the article in easily comprehensible English or the regional language the magazine subscribes to. It needs a specialised command over the area and the subject, and both information and knowledge about ongoing movements taking place in the world of computers. This is precisely the reason that draws top cricketers who have retired from first-class cricket to write columns and articles on the game both in newspapers and in specialised sports magazines."

Writing and Style

So, what does a niche journalist need to do to join such magazines? To begin with, a person aspiring to become a niche journalist has to have all the qualities of a journalist—nose for news, good writing skills, be fast with filing a story and develop reliable news sources. Besides all these qualities, a niche journalist also needs to have expertise in the subject he is writing about. If a journalist is working for a travel magazine, he should not only know about tourism and the destination that he is writing about but also be able to express it clearly in his words. For travel writers it is important that they bring out the flavour of the destination in their story. The story needs to paint the image of sun sets, crowded streets, the aroma of food, busy markets, a sense of history and the writer's delight as being a part of this setting.

At the same time, the travel writer should be able to also fill up the boring parts of the article—how to reach the destination, which hotels to choose, good restaurants to visit and the speciality of the place. Is the town a tourists' delight because it offers a slice of history with museums, forts and palaces, or is it a venue for business conferences, meetings and team-building sessions. On the other hand a destination can be good for sporting and adventure activities like boating, trekking, rafting, hiking, mountain-climbing, rock-climbing and zip-lining while there could be a destination that is suitable for lazying around in the sun, tanning on the beach, reading a book, shopping in the streets and going for a relaxed swim.

With digital technology rendering photography easy, travel journalists now have the added task of taking photographs of their destinations—the towns, cities, markets, sunsets and beaches, mountains, lakes, museums and palaces. Besides these, photographs of food, wines, restaurants, hotels and resorts and the activities that a tourist can indulge himself in that destination have to be taken. With digital photography, can editing and improving the photographs be far behind? So, a travel journalist today is not just a person with a flair for writing, but also one who is good at taking and, sometimes, editing photographs as well.

Some of the top travel magazines in India include *Outlook Traveller, Lonely Planet, National Geographic Traveller, Conde Nast Traveller, Discover India and Travel + Leisure India (T+L).*

Women's magazines occupy one of the biggest segments in niche magazines. And they cover a wide range of topics—fashion, clothes, accessories, hair styles to new-age professions, health, fitness, lifestyle, leisure and women's issues. Women's magazines are replete with advertisements for garments, accessories, jewellery, health products, fitness and lifestyle goods and a wide variety of mindboggling merchandise. This factor, that there is a big separate market for female buyers, many of whom take independent decisions also has been a driver for women-led niche magazines which has fuelled a demand for journalism on women's products and issues.

Women's magazines are not just about shopping and products, these also cater to their needs, emotions, aspirations and ambitions. With women increasingly becoming independent, they confront many problems—work-life balance, sexual harassment at the workplace, office politics, technology, new professions for women, relationships within family and relationships outside of family. There are many other issues to write about—safety in cities and public transport, stalking, health and education for women, combatting stereotypes and fighting sexism. Journalists writing for women's magazines tackle all these diverse issues—ensuring that they maintain the balance between writing on fashion and taking on the challenges faced by working women. A fast-changing world due to media, technology and education is ensuring that these issues have spilled over to rural and the small cities in India where the aspirations of women have risen. Rural women too are fighting their own struggles, some of which are getting featured in women's magazines.

It is true that the majority of the content that appears in women's magazines is related to fashion and lifestyle, movies and models and similar non-serious issues. However, these magazines also have articles that address the concerns of women, mostly young, modern and outgoing women. A journalist writing for a women's magazine will have to be familiar with the humdrum of daily news. Besides that, she has to be aware of women's issues and what goes on in the life of contemporary women in India. The journalist will also have to be updated about films, fashion and food, relationships and careers as well as city life and how urban living impinges upon women.

The market for women's magazines is a crowded one. One of the oldest is *Femina*, brought out by The Times of India group, while the others include almost half-a-dozen foreign publications. *Savvy, Women's Era, Cosmopolitan, Elle India, Good Housekeeping, Verve, Vogue, Grazia* and *Marie Claire* are some of the other main magazines catering to women readers.

In the burgeoning market of niche journalism in India, how can one ignore fashion, films and entertainment magazines which take a large slice of the cake. Their focus is entirely on entertaining the readers instead of providing them with any serious journalistic information. These magazines feature the lives of celebrities, articles on movies, music, lifestyle, society and interviews with superstars. Often, such magazines may slip in a bit of juicy gossip about film and television stars as well.

Then there are niche magazines that specialise in equity, investments, stock markets and shares. Journalists and writers for these magazines have an in-depth understanding of how stock exchanges and financial institutions work. Writing on finance, stocks and trading has become a highly specialised task and not every journalist has the skills to understand markets. Stock markets fluctuate and not even journalists can predict what will happen to markets in the future. In such a situation, the publisher of such a magazine will heavily and wisely depend upon experts to do the writing and analysis of what is happening in the stock exchanges. For example, the *Dalal Street Investment Journal* (DSIJ), which is a fortnightly equity research and capital investment magazine, has a number of experts on markets and the corporate sector who write for it regularly. They may not always be journalists but they provide a diversity of information and correct news about stock market research, capital market analysis, advice on personal finance, views on international markets, analysis of economic activities and their impact on Indian stocks.

With environment and climate change becoming important news aspects, there is an increased focus on these topics as well. *Down To Earth* and *Sanctuary Asia* are two magazines that write extensively on environment and pollution related issues. Journalists writing for such magazines are knowledgeable on topics related to air, land and water pollution besides wildlife, forests, rivers, mountains and deserts. These journalists write about the impacts of climate change and man's relationship with nature. They also analyse in detail how human activities are causing extensive harm to the environment. Such journalists write about government policies as well as international negotiations and politics on environment between the UN and various countries. Journalists writing on environment and development will focus on people's issues like water, agriculture, forestry, mining, livelihoods and how industries impact species and environment in damaging ways.

With specialised magazines on almost every aspect of human life, can magazines on cars, bikes and automobiles be far behind. Vehicles form an important part of people's life and passion. Many would-be journalists join auto magazines to pursue their passion of being close to automobiles. Their job entails reviewing newly-launched vehicles. They test drive the vehicles, make comparative charts and provide easy-to-understand information to their readers. Their job is not just limited to driving vehicles and writing about these. They possess in-depth technical knowledge about the engine, suspension, design, braking systems, lights and many more things. Besides the technical and pricing aspects of vehicles, they are also aware of the auto industry and attend automobile exhibitions and industry fairs.

How should a journalism student choose between writing for niche magazines? The first suggestion that comes to mind is that the journalist should choose a topic that he or she is interested in. Working for a magazine that shares your interests and expertise will allow you to combine your passion and professional quotient. Remember that because you are interested in the subject does not mean that you are qualified to bring justice to your writing. Therefore, you will have to ensure that you are a committed writer by researching your topic, editing, re-writing and improving your story. For a good story, remember to speak with experts and people who are specialists in that subject so that they can provide you with interesting angles and quotes.

Another suggestion for a journalist working for specialised magazines is that the person has to keep himself abreast of the latest trends in their chosen field. This can be done by gleaning information from the internet and also by reading other niche magazines.

NOTES

1. https://www.indiatodaygroup.com/about-us.php
2. https://www.outlookindia.com/magazine/story/a-history-of-ioutlooki/295686
3. https://frontline.thehindu.com/aboutus/

5

Reporting

News Gathering with Integrity

In the opening chapter of this book, *Developing Communication Skills: Fundamentals of Good Writing*, one of the aspects we had discussed was—Language for Reporting. We had explained quite comprehensively the important aspects of writing skills, which a reporter should try to acquire—so essential to achieve even a modicum of success as a journalist. Therefore, a competence to express in written and spoken language is the first basic prerequisite for a journalist—whether a reporter, a feature writer or a sub-editor.

Definitions

The core of reporting is news gathering. A report is a news article for a newspaper or an audio or video recording for radio and TV channels. It gives information about something that has just happened. Reportage is the reporting of news and other events of general interest for newspapers, television or radio. By far the best definition of reporting has been given by George A. Hough, Professor Emeritus, The University of Georgia, who says: Reporting is a journalist's word for research, for the collection of data, for the gathering of facts. This research is topical. It deals with current events, contemporary issues and people. *Reporting is the art, the skill, the business, and the profession of gathering information for immediate use.*

Reporters are the key operators in any news organization—newspapers, wire agencies, magazines, radio and television networks as well as online media. They have also been called the foot soldiers of the news world. A reporter is the primary source of news, the man who "brings it back alive".

Another writer of a communication manual, *The Newsroom*, Frank Barton says: "For no matter how independent, how courageous, even how brilliant the editor's editorials may be, no matter how typographically attractive the subs make a paper appear, at the end of the day it is the news stories the reporters have found and the way they have written them that the paper will be judged."

The reporter has the 'first crack' at the news. He decides how an event is to be presented. He is generally considered the backbone of the news gathering operation.

Eminent journalist M.V. Kamath considers reporters to be a key element in any news organisation. He says: "Let it be said right away a reporter is to a news organisation what a brick is to mansion. A newspaper is what its reporters make of it. The reporter's job, to put it in a nutshell, is to gather news. If he is good at his job, he will work with speed, clarity and accuracy. On these three pillars is erected the whole of the reporter's function in journalism. Speed is the very essence of a reporter's job. Time, tide and news wait for nobody. News delayed is no news, unless no one has had access to it till then. The best reporter is still *Narada* of mythological fame: he was always right where the event was taking place."

Functions and Responsibilities of a Reporter

Apart from having a competent command over the language, a reporter must have a sound general education, preferably with a background of social sciences or humanities. He needs to have a quick enquiring mind, one that is interested in what is going on in the society. Not only that he should also be aware of happenings in his country as well as the world at large, and an innate interest in mankind. A reporter shall have a well-rounded personality—a sense of fairplay and being capable of unbiased approach.

A sound general education will also imply a good knowledge of at least two languages. In India, especially where a large number of languages are spoken, often a reporter with knowledge of more important languages, including the principal regional language of the area where he works, shall have an obvious advantage over others who are not multilingual.

Some of the important qualities essential for a reporter are given below.

(i) *News Sense:* The foremost quality that a journalist must possess is news sense, or what is generally called in the newsroom—*nose for news*. This involves an understanding of news and news values and the ability to recognize a story when it happens. Nose for news is not something one is born with; it is an acquired competence. It can be developed over a period of time and it improves with experience. It also implies a reporter's instincts, which is used to gather information and to make news decisions as early as possible. Experienced reporters often have a good nose for news because they have had long exposure to how editors think and what readers want to read. An experienced reporter would be able to figure out whether a particular story will make it to page one. The three elements, which generally constitute news sense are: instinct, experience and broad knowledge of the news gathering process.

(ii) *Objectivity:* The objective presentation of news is accorded a high ranking in journalism. Walter Lippmann has spoken of the "enduring importance" of objectivity in reporting. He said: "It contains what we may call the Bill of Rights of the working newspaperman. It encourages not only the energetic reporting of facts. It encourages the honest search for truth to which these facts belong. It imposes restraints upon owners and editors. It authorizes resistance, indeed, in honour it calls for resistance to the contamination of news by special prejudices and special interests."

A reporter should not allow his personal bias or ideas to creep into the story. He should not take sides but try to cover different viewpoints while covering a news event.

(iii) *Clarity and Simplicity:* The worst thing that anybody can say about a reporter's story is that it is not clear. If the sub-editor handling the story says this and the reporter is not around to clarify, then the story is more likely to be dropped. The one rule that must never be broken by reporters is clarity. The story must be clear, accurate and so written that the reader can understand it clearly at the first reading.

This case for clarity should apply to everything else in the newspaper news, features, the editorial and even radio and television programmes.

(iv) *Accuracy:* This begins with the reporter's painstaking attention to every detail while gathering facts and information. The credo of Associated Press is: "Good reporters get the facts right. They seek comments from all sides. They check. They do not cut corners." The great American editor and publisher, Joseph Pulitzer, had this motto for his editorial staff: "Accuracy, accuracy, accuracy." He said: "It is not enough to refrain from publishing fake news; it is not enough to avoid the mistakes which arise from ignorance, the carelessness, the stupidity of one or more of the many men who handle the news before it gets into printing. You have got to do much more than that, you have got to make everyone connected with the paper—your editors, your reporters, your correspondents, your rewrite men, your proof-readers—believe that accuracy is to a newspaper what virtue is to a woman."

(v) *Balance and Fairness:* If you are covering a controversial issue, be sure to get across to the people on both sides of the controversy. Getting both sides is the reporter's safeguard against the inaccuracy of the informants involved in the dispute. One-sided stories can also be damaging and legally dangerous. If someone makes an allegation against another person and the newspaper carries the allegation, it is also obliged to carry the response. Fairness requires that the reporter reports the allegations and the response together as far as possible. The *Financial Express* Code of Conduct says: "Whenever we write about a company, and especially if it involves adverse references, we must make every effort to contact the company/its spokesman for their point of view. And, where necessary, we must give the company enough time to respond. It is not right to call-up someone at eight in the night and demand an immediate reply to a complex set of allegations. This is not fair reporting."

In this context, *The Tribune's* Code for Journalists says: "Good faith with the reader is the foundation of good journalism. Every effort must be made to ensure that the news content is accurate, free from bias in context, and that all sides are represented fairly."

(vi) *Scepticism:* A healthy dose of scepticism will always stand a reporter in good stead. Reporters need to be on guard from sources and influences who wish to use him and his paper for planting stories. All sorts of persons—politicians, public relations persons and advertisers come up with bloated claims about the popularity and standing as well as the importance of their institutions and products. All such claims need to be verified through independent and reliable sources.

(vii) *Integrity:* Absolute integrity on the part of a journalist has been enjoined by all news organizations. Integrity implies undeviating honesty and strict adherence to the code of ethics formulated by different news organizations. The Press Council of India has laid down guidelines for journalists working in financial newspapers which say: "The financial journalists should not accept gifts, loans, trips, discounts, preferential shares or other considerations which compromise or are likely to compromise his position." Regarding junkets sponsored by companies or business establishments it says: "When the trips are sponsored for visiting establishments of a company, the author of the report, who has availed of the trip, must state invariably that the visit was sponsored by the company concerned and that it had also extended the hospitality as the case may be."

The Times of India Group's Code of Ethics says: "A journalist who holds shares in a particular company must inform his head of department/editor before writing a story related to the company. Insider trading by a journalist on the basis of privileged information is a gross violation of professional ethics."

Beat Reporting

Beat—Definitions

A journalist's beat is the area which is assigned to him for reporting. Beat is defined as the exclusive territory or a geographical area assigned to a reporter to gather news. Another definition is: "A particular subject or area covered by a reporter for gathering news." Police, Courts, Municipal Council, Government are the examples of beats.

Most of the reporting in newspapers is done by beat reporters. A reporter is assigned to cover a particular beat full time—to gather, organise and write all the news that is generated within the territory or the subject. Some of the common beats in City Reporting, or Metro Reporting, are: Crime and Police; Law and Courts; the City

Government; Municipal Corporation and other Civic Agencies; Urban Development Authorities; Education—universities, schools and colleges; Health—hospitals and medical services.

A reporter should know how things work on his beat. The reporter covering crime should know the police system and the chain of command in the police department. A reporter covering the city government beat should be aware of the working of the education, health and other departments, as well as policies of the administration. A reporter covering health and hospitals should be conversant with the working of hospitals and also problems faced by patients. Only then he will be able to work efficiently even under pressure.

City Reporting

As most of the readers are concentrated in urban areas, newspapers are focusing more on news emanating from the metropolises in a bid to attract readers with local news. The City Desk, headed generally either by the Chief Reporter, or in some cases by the Metro Editor, is a hub of activity for collection of news and keeping tabs on what is happening in the city. Here is a brief description of some of the important beats:

(i) **City Government:** The most important beat in a city is the city government. Every newspaper has at least one reporter assigned to cover the government and its various ministries. The reporter will cover the policies of the government, the constituent assembly, the budget and will also write about the top officials in the city. In the case of Delhi, the reporter will write about the Chief Minister, the Lt. Governor, the Delhi Assembly and all the departments of the Delhi Government.

(ii) **Civic Affairs:** The reporter assigned to local bodies such as a municipal corporation or urban authority is responsible for covering the functioning of the civic bodies. He will analyse and report on matters of local administration, such as development plans, housing schemes, environment, health, road, water, slum and sanitation schemes. Newspapers are the watchdogs against inefficiency, maladministration and corruption in local bodies. The public looks up to them for getting unbiased information related to their area. A reporter must maintain absolute neutrality in reporting civic affairs.

(iii) **Crime:** The police administration in towns has a system for informing the media about traffic, law and order and crime issues. An official is assigned the duty to maintain liaison with the press. In district towns the Superintendent of Police himself maintains contact with the crime reporter. However, in such cases, it would be advisable on his part to cross-verify information with the public.

Sometimes the police will deliberately manipulate crime-related data in a city to show good performance on their part. A reporter is bound to give official figures but if his own enquiries reveal that the official figures are wrong, it is his duty to point this out. These days there is a tendency to sensationalize reporting crime. There have been instances wherein after some murder, the newspaper headline was "Welcome to the crime capital of India". Such sensationalism must be avoided at all costs. While writing about crime, it is essential to be fair and accurate. In case the reporter is not sure about facts, he may qualify his information by writing 'alleged', 'suspected' and by quoting officials. Speculation regarding guilt or innocence should always be avoided.

(iv) **Education:** The education beat gives a reporter good stories. The education system has been expanding rapidly—government education departments at the state level, universities, scientific and research institutes at the central level and also the school system. The student and teacher unions always come up with their demands and problems which are a source of news. Research studies conducted by various departments in universities are a potential stories. Parents also want issues like increase in school fees, improving quality of education and government policies to be highlighted in the media.

(v) **Health and Environment:** A reporter covering these issues will have hospitals, health research institutes and medical colleges as his beat. The issues that he will cover will include health policies of the government, outbreaks of disease like malaria, dengue or cholera, administration of hospitals, malpractices in government hospitals, overbilling or wrong diagnosis in private hospitals and innovations in medical research.

The health reporter also writes on environment issues as these are interrelated. On the environment front a reporter will write about air pollution and growing incidence of respiratory illnesses, the state of parks and green areas in the city, the quality of potable water, groundwater levels in the city and increase or decrease in green areas. The reporter will get news and information from doctors, patients, NGOs besides government officials.

(vi) **General Assignment Reporter:** A general assignment reporter is not assigned to a particular beat. He is also called a Cub Reporter and is asked to write on a wide range of news events. While the beat reporter has a specific geographical area or a particular subject to cover, a general assignment reporter may be deputed to an assignment which suddenly crops up. He should be able to write quickly and under pressure.

Types of News Reporting

The media has expanded and diversified so much that different forms of news reporting have evolved, with each form developing its own characteristics and distinctive features. Some of the important types of news reporting are given below:

Political Reporting: Political reporting includes reporting activities, conferences and events concerning political parties. Major political parties at the national level, and even in the states, generally have party spokespersons who regularly brief reporters about the point of view of the party on various issues of governance. Parties hold press conferences to release their manifestos, explain their policies and strategies for the election. In any news organisation political reporting enjoys a high degree of importance. In India, reporting politics has been a major preoccupation with the media—a legacy from the pre-independence days. A political correspondent knows leaders of major political parties, has access to ministers and senior politicians; and is not only reporting political events but also analyzing them. With regional political parties playing an important role at the national level, political reporting from state capitals has become important.

This kind of reporting sometimes tends to take the shape of political propaganda. Several journalists tend to become closely associated with a particular political party so much that they become openly partisan. Propaganda is an organized effort to propagate a doctrine, a concept or a campaign. It does not generally have ethical content. Ever since electoral politics has assumed prominence, political reporting has come into its own. The party manifestos—with best possible postulates including growth and development, social justice, fighting communalism, rural development, health, education, in short issues which would go down well with the electorate, are publicised. The spokespersons of political parties are in touch with the media, particularly political reporters, for getting across their point of view. A reporter must not be seen as being a part of propaganda by being associated too closely with a political party.

The quality and norms of political reporting will depend on the nature of the political system in which a reporter operates. In a truly democratic country, journalists will enjoy a great measure of freedom in interpretation and analysis.

Political reporting is the most complex of the genres of reporting requiring detailed knowledge about governance and policies as well as deep understanding of political parties and personalities. The dependable rule for the reporter is to be non-partisan and to guard himself against being drawn into a controversy. While covering a national meeting of a political party, the reporter will have to explain not only what decisions are reached at the meeting but also whether they represent any variation from the party's past policy and what effect these decisions are likely to have on the party's future.

Senior journalist, S. Nihal Singh, says: "It is not a reporter's job to further his own political philosophy or bias by tilting to one party or politician or the other. It is his job to assess a situation as objectively as he can, draw his conclusions from a rigorous examination of the often contradictory assertions he has gathered and, based upon his experience and study, present an honest picture of the trend."

The most difficult aspect of political reporting is to strike a balance in a reporter's relationship with a politician. By the nature of his job, he must cultivate politicians and be privy to their confidences.

Science Reporting: Science and technology are shaping mankind as never before and it is increasingly necessary for society to know what are scientists working on. A dialogue between scientists and the public is possible only if the knowledge gap between them is narrowed through science reporting which is easy to understand. This is a vital function of science journalism in modern society.

Science is too vast and specialization in one field does not make the reporter a specialist in other fields of science. But specialization does help in the sense that it exposes a science reporter to the methods of science, the techniques used by scientists, and the conditions under which research is done. This enables a journalist to communicate effectively news and information on science, research and technology to the public.

It is essential that the reporter has a background in science and a temperament that encourages constant learning about the beat that he is covering. New knowledge is being generated everyday, therefore, a reporter has to keep himself aware of the major developments happening in different disciplines to spot a good story.

The growing importance of science and technology in everyday life is obvious as more and more people are using gadgets and newer forms of technology. Catering to increasing public interest in technological changes, the space provided to this fascinating field by newspapers and magazines is increasing day by day.

Science writing in newspapers and periodicals is entirely different from articles published in specialized journals. The writer needs to make the subject comprehensible to a layperson. One difficulty that the scientists face is that they fail to make the subject lucid and interesting. Here lies the challenge for a science reporter—make the topic easy to comprehend for the general public. A reporter has to go out of his way to de-jargonise and explain scientific and technical phenomenon in simple language.

The first lesson that every science and technology journalist should remember is: Give the reader the subject in everyday language and he will become a friend for life.

In the context of science reporting, one practical suggestion is to talk about the everyday use of the subject in the very beginning. The common reader is interested in knowing how your article will impact his life. Illustrations and pictures are absolutely essential to this branch of writing. These not only explain the subject better but are also pleasing to the eye.

Sports Reporting: In most newspapers, the sports page is one of the most popular pages, particularly for the young readership. During big sporting events like the Olympics, the Commonwealth Games, the

Asian Games, world cup cricket, international tennis tournaments or the football world cups, it is not unusual for normal activities to come to a standstill as people remain glued to their television sets.

The best sports reporting captures the atmosphere as well as the facts of the game. But remember that the reader wants to know the facts first.

Big sporting events today have rules and celebrity players. The reporter must know about these rules and should be able to reach out to the star players for exclusive quotes. He must know which players are in form or have not done well and also the past performance of the teams. The sports reporter must, therefore, do as much research as he can before the game starts and should quickly file his story.

A good sports reporter knows the players, the manager and the officials. The personal lives of sportsmen are matters of great public interest, especially since their earnings put them among the big spenders whose homes, families and cars are of much public interest. As sport persons are increasingly taking to endorsing commercial products, and have been the subject of match-fixing controversies, public interest in their professional performance, personal life and family background has naturally increased.

The sports writer is different from the general reporter in one respect: he is at the same time a reporter and a critic. He is giving his opinion about the game at the same time as he is describing the facts. He also judges the quality and skill of the players.

Each sport has its own jargon and special terms. Avoid using jargon without explaining it for the benefit of readers who may not be familiar with the game. Most readers of the sports pages will probably be familiar with the rules and jargon of major sports, such as football and cricket—but never assume that they are.

Television commentary on sports basically follows the rules for newspaper sports reporting, but with a few hazards. The commentator must be aware that the viewers are seeing the sports spectacle with him and should not succumb to the temptation of describing the obvious. The introduction of cameras and advanced technology, along with slow-motion replays, that are played immediately after the incident, has made the job of a sports journalist easy.

It is easy enough to report sport adequately, it requires inspiration and great care to report it really well, write Geoffrey Harris and David Spark in *Practical Newspaper Reporting*. Sport is an area where the pressure of deadlines and comparatively restricted content of each sporting activity make really first class writing difficult to achieve. Yet modern journalism is noted for its great sports writing.

Business Reporting: Since 1970s, business reporting has seen dramatic growth. Earlier, financial dailies existed only in Mumbai, and there were a handful of economic journals, none of which could claim a large circulation.

Since then business reporting has moved out of the back waters of journalism into the mainstream. There are financial dailies from major cities—Mumbai, Delhi, Kolkata, Chennai, Bangalore and Ahmedabad. *The Economic Times* today has one of the largest circulations among all English-language business newspapers in the country. *The Financial Express, Mint, Business Standard* and *The Businessline* are the other prominent business and financial newspapers in the country. This segment also has a number of news magazines like *Business India, Business Today, Outlook Business* and many others. The general purpose newspapers too have increased considerably their economic and commercial coverage.

In U.S.A. the *Wall Street Journal*, usually counted as a general circulation newspaper, is actually the largest and the most influential newspaper in this segment. Another well-known business magazine is *Fortune*, whose rankings of the largest companies, called Fortune 500 are widely quoted. Some of the world's greatest newspapers—such as *The Times* or the *New York Times* have large and regular business sections to cater to a significant section of their readership.

Business reporting includes writing about government policy, corporates, banking, finance, agriculture, industry, the share market, trade and the budget. Each of these segments encompasses numerous micro-segments. For example, a reporter writing on agriculture will also cover areas like food and commercial crops, agricultural research, irrigation, fertilizers and agro-industries. Similarly, rural development encompasses not only agriculture but also several related occupations, electrification, water, health and different aspects of infrastructure.

The broad indicators of a country's economy consist of the growth rates in national income, the growth rates in agriculture and industry, exports and imports, wholesale and retail prices, bank deposits and advances and the rate of money supply expansion, foreign exchange reserves and the balance of payments position. Familiarity with economic terms is essential. The reporter who does not know the difference between per capita income and gross national product is going to have trouble. A dictionary of economic terms would be a handy tool to resolve some of these difficulties.

The changing direction of economic policy has made business journalism a subject of interest for a layman. The policy of economic liberalization ushered in July 1991 through a comprehensive economic package which focused among others on correcting the external value of rupee, delicensing industrial sector, liberalization and de-bureaucratizing import licensing system led to the development and expansion of business journalism.

With greater influence of corporatisation and globalization on national policies, business journalism has created a significant and important place for itself.

It will not be out of context to make a mention of the writing style of Nobel Laureate Amartya Sen. His book, *India—Development and Participation*, discusses issues like economic reforms and policies in a language and style which makes the subject clear and easy even for a non-specialist reader. It is, therefore, essential for a business reporter to adopt a writing style which his readers will find easy to understand even on topics related to annual budget, deficit financing and other such terms.

Parliamentary Reporting: In a democratic country like India, the Parliament and the legislatures in different states, enjoy a special position of importance and prestige. These bodies are the law makers of the country and give directions to the governments both at the Centre and the states. They also transact important business, like presentation of the budget and sanction grants to individual ministries. The debates in these bodies, particularly in Parliament, are read with interest by the people. Sometimes, matters are discussed in the Parliament through Adjournment Motion. The debates on individual ministries also evoke great interest.

Since proceedings of the Parliament, reflect the working not only of the government, but also of other political parties, the reporter not only reports the proceedings but also provides an analysis and background of the happenings in the Parliament.

Since the Parliament has its own rules of procedure, conventions and privileges, breach of any of these may create problems for the parliamentary reporter. It is, therefore, essential that a parliament report should be accurate in identification of the members by name, party affiliation and constituency. He has to be careful in reporting proceedings of the Parliament, particularly cases in which the presiding officer of the House may expunge either some remarks of the members or portions of the proceedings of the day. In India, under the Parliament Proceedings Act, 1956, the press is privileged to publish proceedings of Parliament and State legislatures without fear of legal action. Parliamentary reporting includes important events as Budget Presentation, Motions of Thanks to the President, and important policy announcements.

In reporting Parliament, sometimes, the newspapers are criticized for giving too much prominence to statements by members of the ruling party. To some extent, this is unavoidable because the ruling party is in majority and more of its members will naturally be quoted by journalists. Therefore, it is essential that the views of opposition members be also reported with the same care.

Investigative Reporting: The work of a reporter involves certain amount of investigation, enquiry or examination of facts and details. He has to explore and get into various aspects of an incident or occurrence. Investigative journalism involves finding out the truth. One of the popular definitions of news by William Randolph Hearst says: "News is something, someone, somewhere wants suppressed. All rest is advertising."

Ever since the two enterprising reporters of *The Washington Post*, Carl Bernstein and Bob Woodward committed themselves to unravelling the Watergate scandal, which ultimately led to the resignation of U.S. President Richard Nixon, investigative journalism got a boost. However, the idea that this type of reporting is relatively new and became important only as a result of Watergate era of 1970s is a misconception. Journalists have always been society watchdogs and have involved themselves in investigating wrongdoings. Quite often they have to go to great lengths to ferret out well-guarded information.

Investigative reporting is generally a job to be undertaken carefully and thoroughly over a period of time. The two reporters devoted nearly every waking hour to the case during the period between the burglary and the election of President Nixon for months. They went at night to the homes of the staff members of the re-election campaign committee, would ask questions and go back repeatedly with more queries. Despite hostility and denials from the White House staff, they did not give up the investigation. It was hard work, straight reporting all through.

Interestingly Bob Woodward, now popularly nicknamed "Watergate Woodward," an assistant managing editor at *The Washington Post*, has released *Bush at War* which offers a new insight into the tensions that afflicted President Bush's War Cabinet during the initial stages of the Afghanistan War in November 2001. Woodward's sources divulge to him the inner workings of the Bush government. A review of the book says about Woodward: "He lives by the leak, and the leaks are here in ample supply—memos and records of National Security Council meetings, alongside his interviews with the principals."

Personal Integrity and Motivation an Absolute Must for Investigative Journalism: According to Clark Mollenhoff, the doyen of investigative reporting in the US, personal integrity and motivation for the investigative reporter is essential for the craft. Any action by the reporter or the newspaper that are illegal, politically partisan, or even unfair by generally accepted standards can undercut or destroy a valid journalistic inquiry. *The investigative reporters must believe that it pays to be honest and ethical and know that any illegality or dishonesty is dangerous for the reporter, the newspaper, and the cause in which they are interested.* He makes it clear that sources and the public will be disillusioned if the reporter or newspaper misuses the power and intentionally distorts the picture or engages in superficial sensationalism. Investigative reporting may be reflective, even speculative but always based on hard-core evidence.

In India, several intrepid young reporters have laid bare the sordid happenings in public domain—jail administration, stock market, as also defence deals etc. In order to investigate wretched conditions in the Tihar Central Jail, Ashwini Sarin of *The Indian Express* got himself arrested on a flimsy charge and refused bail. The paper carried four of his investigative reports on the inside story of Tihar Jail. Likewise

Sucheta Dalal formerly of *The Times of India*, while going through the stock market quotations, noticed phenomenal rise in the value of shares. Her patient investigation revealed manipulation of the market by a stock broker in connivance with stock exchange and Indian and foreign banks. Arun Shourie, who during his stewardship of *The Indian Express*, has made the newspaper the cutting edge of opposition to the government tackled issues like corruption, prison reforms, bonded labour, the plight of under trials through sustained investigation and the hard team work. When he wrote of the Muslim Women Bill he had read the *Quran*, the *Hadith*, the parables of the Prophet so that he could not be faulted for superficiality.

The series, *The Great Indian Bank Robbery*, published in 2002 by Ritu Sarin and Sucheta Dalal, exposed the wrongdoings indulged in by the Indian business and industry, and the tactics it resorts to in not paying back huge loans it owes to public sector banks. Similarly, the investigation into the Bofors case in 1987 by the Chennai-based *The Hindu* newspaper by Chitra Subramaniam and N. Ram has gone down as one of the finest pieces of investigative journalism in India. Again in 2001, *Tehelka* magazine exposed the wrongdoings in defence deals. All these investigative stories had far reaching impact on governance and many led to changes in laws and policy. It is clear that investigative journalism takes time, persistence and discipline for a reporter and often is the result of team work. Also, this type of reporting is performing an extremely significant public service function.

Gender Issues Reporting: Gender issues have been held centre stage for close to four decades or more. There have been numerous news reports, features, articles, books, publications on women empowerment and other related subjects. The Fourth UN Conference on Women (Beijing, 1995) devoted a separate section to 'Women and the Media', in the final Declaration and Platform for Action adopted at the conclusion of the Conference. It clearly defined the significant role media needed to play in accelerating the process of advancement of women.

Gender issues include all those areas which concern women's personal and social well-being. Amenities provided by the state for the comfort of its women citizens, and the steps taken by different organizations for improving the quality of women's lives are women issues, as much as the prevalent social apathy towards violence against women and the ongoing efforts to invite women to participate at various levels of administration.

There are several reasons for gender issues being increasingly reported in the press: Representation of women in Panchayati Raj institutions, leading role being performed by women activists in areas of environmental protection (Chipko movement) and other such campaigns, increased awareness regarding atrocities and violence against women, and improved women literacy. The writings and philosophy of Nobel Laureate Amartya Sen regarding gender inequality and women's agency, as well as on female deprivation has created new awakening on this subject. A number of institutions like National Women Commission and women study centres provide reports and research findings which constitute a rich source of information for reporters. Another reason for greater coverage of gender issues in the media is the increasing numbers of female journalists in newsrooms and television studios. However, reporting on gender issues is still considered 'soft news'; as against parliamentary or political reporting.

Interpretative Reporting: The term interpretative reporting means that the reporter seeks to find the implications of an event. The reporter puts the event in perspective and explains, interprets and analyses the event, which goes beyond the strict ambit of his duty as a reporter.

A Manual for News Agency Reporters explains: Analytical reporting is a variation of interpretative writing. It concentrates on events and the trends they may represent, instead of attempting to indicate what they portend. The requirement here, again, is a full understanding of the subject and the related development. In a budget report, for example, the reporter would be required to explain the various components of the budget, how they related to each other, and how they differ from past budgets. Analysis and interpretation differ fundamentally from news reports in that they deal with concepts, while news reports confine themselves to facts. Analysis and interpretation seek to impart a deeper understanding of the processes of which isolated manifestations alone get noticed as news events. Interpretative reporting and news analysis are becoming common genre of reporting these days. Quite often, the analysis also is written even as the events are reported.

Dos and Don'ts for a Reporter

(i) *Reporter's Tools:* A reporter must maintain a standard size notebook, which can be conveniently kept in a pocket. A good reporter will keep a file on everybody he knows, or ought to know, along with correct addresses and telephone numbers, so that he can, at a moment's notice, get in touch with them for information, comment or reaction. He should also maintain a forward diary. A forward diary is one in which he can enter information of events to come.

(ii) A reporter should never take anything for granted. He should never be shy of asking questions. Asking questions is his job.

(iii) *Check and Double Check:* Many reporters get into trouble because they do not bother to check and double check their stories. News sources are sometimes erratic. Therefore, it is essential for a reporter to verify the correct position with respect to a happening. A reporter will do well to remember what Sir John Reith, the first Director General of the BBC, had said in this context: "It is bad to miss a deadline but worse not to have checked the story properly."

(iv) Keep confidence of your sources. If you let down your contact, you lose an important source of information for all times to come.

(v) Always maintain a high level of integrity. Newspapers may sometimes tolerate an incompetent reporter, but never the one whose integrity becomes doubtful.

NOTES

1. Refer to Chapter 2 – *News: Nature and Structure*, p. 21.
2. *The Newsroom, Communication Manual*, Friedrich Ebert Stiftung, Bonn.
3. *Modern Newspaper Practice*, P.W. Hodgson.

REFERENCES

Indian Institute of Mass Communication (1977): *A Manual for News Agency Reporters*, Allied Publishers Private Limited, New Delhi.

Mark Tully and Gillian Wright (2002): *India in Slow Motion*, Penguin Books, New Delhi.

The Media Foundation (1996): *Beyond Those Headlines*, New Delhi.

6

Art of Interviewing

News Gathering in a Different Way

An important skill involved in communication and reporting is the art of interviewing. To report or to communicate news effectively and correctly, requires gathering information which can only be done through the three input sources of seeing, listening and reading.

One of the ways to gather news and information is the interview. It is a basic skill that needs to be understood and mastered for good reporting. Most of the news stories are based on facts gained by asking questions. News features are supported by interviews of experts and news is generally based on references to different persons and personalities. Therefore, we must never underestimate the importance of interviewing which is fundamental to obtaining information.

The term 'interview' is derived from the French word 'entreveue' which means 'to see one another'. It is a meeting between two persons with a specific purpose. It may be defined as any purposeful interpersonal communication between two individuals. An interview demands direct and dynamic interaction. One of the purposes of the interview is to elicit information, which is not available from written records or other sources. There are different types of interviews ranging from the one conducted by a journalist for news gathering to that of a patient by a psychiatrist.

An interview is an exchange of information between a reporter and a source. It is considered as the first resort of all journalists on which a large number of stories appearing in the newspapers are based. A journalist with *The Hindu* says: Good reporting is 80 per cent interviewing.

Conducting a good interview means being prepared. Your background research should include gathering information that can help you to identify the many aspects of the event or issue on which you are working. Just as there is no one definitive way to interview, there is no one way to research. You may have to spend a lot of time in the library or reading through news clipping and books in the office or surfing the web. You may have to make several phone calls or even undertake preliminary discussions with people who can give you background information. Good research also means that you will go into your interview with the idea of what you want to get out of it. Thorough background work should prepare you to understand as much technical information as possible.

If a potential interview involves discussion of a particular event at a site, you should try to visit the site first to get a good mental picture of it. This will help you to formulate questions and make you aware when an interviewee's answers conflict with something you have observed first hand. You should consider, if necessary, preparing an interview schedule or a questionnaire to help you. Interviewing requires patience, confidence and an ability to listen, participate, observe and absorb. Reporters must be able to ask a question and then listen to the entire response, all the time concentrating on the key points.

Three-fourth of an interview is only listening

—Tim Sebastian

Tim Sebastian, former BBC anchor of *Hard Talk*, Badshah of all Talk Shows, in an interview with Nikhat Kazmi, in *The Times of India*, 16 April, 2000, says that three-fourth of an interview is only listening.

Some Interesting Excerpts from the Interview

Surprisingly, people want to share their stories. All you have to do is push at the door and it will open. You know, it's funny how people keep talking about the art of interviewing but they don't realize three-fourths of an interview is only listening. Only one-fourth is about talking. And sometimes, you've got to let the long silences remain because silences can be very telling too. You don't have to fill the entire programme with talk.

Essentially, you've got to create moments of great intimacy with people you have never met.

The rich, the famous, the powerful: do you ever feel intimidated at the prospect of grilling them. Any butterflies in your stomach?

I am always nervous before an interview. But that's not because I'm talking to certain people. No, I have always been nervous about broadcasting. Do you know I was a shy little schoolboy who was terrified of reading out loud in class?

As the Hard Talker, do you envisage your role as an interrogator, a friend, a counsel or an inquisitor?

I see myself as a catalyst who is trying to get people to talk about themselves in the most effective way. Now I have to find the key to unlock the person sitting in front of me. Rarely can you unlock the front door, which is always closely guarded. So you've got to go in through the back or side door and somehow, find a key for it. You see, interviewing is not an exact science. It is largely intuitive. You have to engage with the other person, and it's impossible to engage with everybody. People aren't robots. People aren't computers.

Art of the Interview

People think that interviewing is easy, that it's simply a matter of going somewhere and asking someone a few questions. Anyone with a little nerve can do that. The truth, however, is that to interview is an art, and a difficult one. Let us think first of all what the interview is for. News interviews and feature interviews have different objectives, but in general you want four things from them:

Information: Hard fact: What happened, where did you go, what are your plans, how much will it cost. And give examples to illustrate your theme.
Quotes: To add authority, colour and impact.

Authority: It's harder to disbelieve named, quoted sources speaking in their own words.
Colour: The quality of language. Speech is more flexible than formal writing. Direct quotes can give more of the flavour of a personality. Good interviewers—particularly feature writers—use their eyes and their ears for more than just words. They look for details in the interviewee's clothes, environment, and mannerisms. These things add life and perspective to the story.
Impact: Good use of quotes helps lift out the key points. It can emphasize a telling statement or reflect a mood.

The aim of an interview is to provide, in the interviewee's own words, facts, reasons or opinions on a particular topic so that the listener can form a conclusion as to the validity of what she/he is saying. The opinions of the interviewer are not to be counted here and he should not get drawn into answering the question himself/herself. Within the present definition, it is the interviewee who must come through in the programme and not the interviewers.

Examples of Interesting Interviews

Here are some examples of interesting interviews published in newspapers and magazines. These have been selected out of a large number of interviews for being interesting, informative and of human interest value.

'Time and Time Again', *South China Morning Post, 4 April 2001.*

Ah Wong, 28 times convict narrates his story of more than thirty years behind bars. It is not that he likes it to be in prison. All he ever wanted were a stable home and life, but the unemployment, homelessness and loneliness that greet him outside the penitentiary gates eventually also send him back inside.

> *Ah Wong, like many of these men (and more than 84 per cent of these prisoners are men), looks nothing like the stereotypical "bad guy" or "hardened criminal". He has a wide smile, an easy*

manner and is almost sheepish when asked about his youth and all the mistakes he has made.

He was troubled from the beginning. Born into a poor but very large family, he says he received little attention from anyone unless and until he got into trouble. He did badly at school and with little to hold on to at home, Ah Wong found a new family in his friends on the streets. He says he was "just hanging out" until an experiment with heroin sent him to a boy's home at 15. "Once I got into drugs, I just got really lazy. All we would do was hang around. I was not interested in working but needed money for the drugs, so we would steal and do whatever we could to get it," Ah Wong says.

His family disowned him as "a good-for-nothing" and after that there was no turning back. Drugs and petty thefts have made sure that he never gets too far from the prison gates. But after more than 30 years, he still yearns for a job and a stable home. Asked what his dream is, Ah Wong says simply: "I would wish for a job."

This interview is a major part of the feature, Time and Time Again, published in the features section of *the Hong Kong* daily. The feature has interviews with several other persons: a number of ex-convicts, a senior clinical psychologist for the Correctional Services Department, a social worker from the Society for the Rehabilitation of Offenders, Hong Kong (SROHK), and a representative from a voluntary group, Prisoners' Friends' Association.

The interviews discuss the problems of rehabilitation of ex-offenders, crime prevention and the role of Non-Governmental Organizations. The interviews draw a graphic picture of living conditions in the prison. Written in a straightforward, direct style the feature lets the interviewees express themselves freely.

There are very few intrusions from the writer—a hallmark of a really good journalism. Along with interviews the feature has a simple graphics of line drawings depicting prison doors. An example of first rate interview and the techniques employed therein.

Interviews are conducted for different purposes and reported in different styles. Some of these are:

(i) Personal Interview: Generally the interviews appearing in newspapers, magazines, radio or television programmes are of important and well-known personalities. The traditional format of such interviews is to give word-for-word answers to the questions. Even the actions of the interviewees are sometimes described in reporting such interviews.

(ii) Interviewing for a Story: Interviewing for a story is common in reporting news and views. The source of all news is some individual. It is quite unlikely that the reporter is present at the site of news except while reporting formal ceremonies. Even actual happening cannot be studied without seeking information from different sources. For instance, you may visit a drought affected or flood hit area, but to know the real story you will have to seek information from the people actually suffering from the impact of such happenings, the government officials engaged in relief work and other agencies working in the area. For these interviews, advance preparation has to be made. The persons to be contacted have to be identified and appointments fixed. The interview is to be conducted in the same way as a personal interview, the most important point to be kept in mind in such cases is to seek the view point of all the concerned parties. This may also involve rechecking information.

Write the story immediately while the interview is still fresh in your mind. While doing so you have to recollect and reflect on the interview and also to check notes and omissions, and anything that is inconsistent. You will do well to remember that it is the story that is important, so use quotes to illustrate important points. Such interviews can provide several related stories and you may decide on the method of reporting them.

(iii) Interviewing for a Feature: Just as information is sought for news and views story, you may need to interview people for writing a feature. It is important to decide on the topic for the feature carefully. Features must be timely and of interest to the readers. A feature on indiscipline on the academic campus will have more relevance when some glaring incident takes place. Features can be on social problems and matters of topical interest like environment and sustainability. A careful research is to be carried out on the subject before writing the feature. Based on this preparation, interviews are conducted with concerned experts or those directly affected. Such interviews provide support to the feature and also make the feature more interesting and informative.

(iv) Interviewing Farmers: Farming constitutes the bedrock of Indian economy even now. Farmers are directly affected by problems like floods and drought, food shortages, natural calamities and interviewing them requires a different treatment and technique. Although farmers are like other persons but they attach more importance to traditions due to social and cultural factors. Interviews of farmers are very useful in writing success stories that encourage other farmers in the region. Such an interview provides real feedback to scientists and extension agencies about the research and development programmes being executed, and also helps develop greater insight in the field problems in agriculture and rural development.

The primary consideration in interviewing farmers is to approach them with sincerity and respect. There is always a lot to learn from them. However, it is difficult to meet them on prefixed appointment, like other professionals. It is important that care is taken to build good rapport with them before the interview. Questions on social and cultural matters should be carefully worded to avoid ridicule or embarrassment to the interviewee.

Guidelines for Interviews

- Always seek an appointment for an interview. Also indicate the amount of time it is likely to take. Go prepared with a notebook as well as a recorder to record the conversation. In case you have a questionnaire prepared, do not always insist that the questionnaire be filled in there and then.
- Preparation for the interview may also include selection of time and place. Often, reporters have no choice: they must interview the person at the airport terminal, the politician in a busy corridor, the executive in a crowded hotel room, the

protest leader in a noisy street. But whenever possible, try to avoid such situations.

- Make sure your questions are clear. Avoid constructing 'leading questions' that steer the interviewee towards a predetermined answer.
- Always ask just one question at a time, not one with two or more parts, and keep your questions short. Even for a brief interview, question should be carefully prepared to make the best possible use of the time. Your purpose is not primarily to fill gaps in your own knowledge, but to find out what your readers would want to know, things which the person is most fitted to tell you.
- A study shows that the person who gets the most answers is simply the person who asks the most questions. And experience demonstrates that the quality of the questions is equally important. A large number of answers are of little value if they are irrelevant to the main subject.
- If a large number of questions have elicited a 'no' response, mould your questions in a way that these elicit proper answers.
- Arrange your questions in an order you think will make for a good conversation, build a rapport with the interviewee and elicit good answers.

Dos and Don'ts

(i) We have to win the trust of our interviewees before anything else. Then we have to make sure that an informant's trust is not violated. It has to be won with effort and sincerity. Your attitude and your words have to instill confidence in the interviewee, and your behaviour and actions during and after the interview have to reflect the confidence you have won.

(ii) Journalism is about forging relationship and relations are about people. So, as in any relationship being sensitive to the situation is the key. A smile, a nod, a laugh or just a touch of hand goes towards building of trust. Sometimes, it is silence that makes other persons realize that you share their grief and you understand their feelings.

Often, if you simply ask, 'tell me what happened,' people will begin to pour out their stories without much more prompting, and you can ask for clarification or more detail from time to time. They may well include many confusing and irrelevant details, but those can be sorted out later. Just sitting and listening to someone's story can be helpful to them as well as giving you an important/initial basis for your story.

(iii) Let the person talk at her own pace and in her own style. Don't hurry her, don't appear hurried yourself and don't try to influence her style of talking. There will be much in what she says which will not go into the final story but be respectful—listen her out. The selection of facts, the editing, the chiseling of sentences and paragraphs can be kept for later.

(iv) Therefore, the words a reporter should choose for his story shall show reporter's attitude. It is the ability to share another person's feelings and emotions as if they were your own. If you empathise with someone, you understand the situation, problems and feelings, because you have been in a similar situation. Empathy is the most important thing in reporting. The reporter may never meet the interviewee again, but for that brief moment when their paths do cross, there should be a feeling of sharing emotions.

(v) In these days of violence, terrorism and large-scale abuse, reporters are frequently assigned the duty to interview the victims of such happenings. A reporter covering case of human rights violations soon discovers that it is often very difficult to know the true story. How do you investigate allegations of abuses in a highly polarized atmosphere, where each person you interview seems to have a vested interest in telling you only a part of the story? Because people are often extremely emotional in these situations, and because they may often not be eye-witnesses to the abuse, it is not always easy to determine fact from rumour. Sometimes, a question must be asked in several different ways, again always trying to respect the feelings of the person being interviewed, who may well have just lost a husband, son, or other close relatives.

(vi) Interviewing children who have undergone trauma is a

ticklish issue. Again, the basic rule applies: Don't begin the conversation with a direct query on the child's horrible experience. Find another, more humane way to start.

(vii) Cultural sensitivity is important. Sharing a cup of tea, a meal, a joke are often preludes to sharing confidences. It relaxes the interviewee. People want to be treated first and foremost as individuals and not as commodities, so your interviewee is not there simply to provide you with a story.

(viii) Read interviews in newspapers and magazines written by well-known journalists. Some of these interviews are reported in the question-and-answer format. Some are titled as 'Face to Face'. Watch interviews being conducted on television. These will help you imbibe the techniques of interviewing.

REFERENCES

Bruce D. Itule and Douglas A. Anderson (1994): *News Writing and Reporting for Today's Media*, McGraw-Hill, Inc., New York.

Kamath, M.V. (1980): *Professional Journalism*, Vikas Publishing House Pvt. Ltd., New Delhi.

Press and People (2001): *A Manual of Human Rights Reporting in India*, British Council Division, New Delhi.

7

Feature Writing

Making News Reader-friendly

Newspapers, traditionally, have been allocating a major portion of their resources and efforts to newsgathering, particularly, hard news. However, during the last three decades the newspapers have seen bold and dramatic changes in terms of content, design, addition of colour and presentation of news.

Since the advent of 24-hour news channels on television, breaking news has become an almost everyday practice. Live news coverage, as the events unfold, has altogether changed the practice of news gathering as never before. The accent now is not simply on what happened—the hard news—but increasingly on the how and the why—the exploration of detail and the human angle, which clearly bring home the point of the story, and place it in context.

Features are increasingly becoming an important part of print media. Newspapers and magazines have taken to features as never before because these have generated a new readership. Feature articles have become so ubiquitous that these are no longer a part of Sunday or magazine journalism alone which had been the established practice till the eighties.

Broad Contours of a Feature

However important a feature may be in the context of present-day journalism, it still defies a precise definition. The following elucidation from different sources should help you understand the broad contours of a feature:

The Collins Cobuild English Dictionary for Advanced Learners says: "A feature is a special article in a newspaper or magazine, or a special programme on radio or television."

In their book, *News Writing and Reporting for Today's Media*, Itule and Anderson say: "Feature is an umbrella term for a number of soft news stories that profile, humanise, add colour, educate, entertain or illuminate." A feature is not meant to deliver news first hand. It usually recaps major news that was reported in a previous news cycle. It can stand alone, or it can be a sidebar to the main story. A sidebar runs next to the main story or elsewhere in the same edition, providing an audience with additional information on the same topic.

One of the best interpretations of the term has been given by late journalist M.V. Kamath in his book, *Professional Journalism*: What is there about a feature which makes it attractive to the readers? Contrary to some belief, it is its timeliness. A feature to be read and appreciated must have immediate reference to what the reader knows only sketchily. A feature, in the circumstances, must fill in the reader with new information of which he has been hitherto ignorant. It must provide him with all that he wanted to know but had no time to enquire about.

A feature is expected to give the background to the news, which includes analysis, explanation and discussion. It should document facts, possibly anticipate developments. As an illustration Kamath says that when it was reported that there had been a sudden spurt in cases of jaundice in Bombay city, *The Illustrated Weekly of India* commissioned a distinguished medical practitioner to write about why and how jaundice strikes and what remedial measures could be taken to prevent its occurrence.

While newspapers present brief write-ups on events, issues and people, features present detailed analysis, often in the form of discussions and narratives. News reports are written mostly in the inverted pyramid formal structure and style, features follow the structures of essays and discussions and present a distinct point of view. A feature, therefore, is an essay like a piece written for publication in a newspaper or magazine. News reports dominate in a newspaper, but in magazines features take up most of the space.

Feature articles are generally longer and are not constrained by a hard news peg, although they still need some element of timeliness.

They vary in length from stories that consist of just one page with a large illustration to a feature that could be several pages long. Writers do not use the standard writing formula and need not place conclusions first because the editor does not often cut from the end of the story. While hard news attempts to tell what is happening, features have more room to develop and provide more perspective.

Importance of Features

There are several reasons why features have become an important part of journalism:

(i) The exponential growth of satellite television in India, and more importantly, proliferation of round-the-clock television news channels, has made sure that the public gets hard news at the earliest—almost at the same time as the event is happening. Newspaper readers wish to read more background articles and in-depth stories which puts the news in a proper perspective.
(ii) The rising percentage of literacy and improvement in educational standards has made even ordinary citizens more aware about the national and international issues. They need information in detail and depth.
(iii) The democratic set-up of society, by its very nature, calls for greater accountability from the elected representatives. Readers are naturally interested to know more about how the taxpayers' money is being spent on public works. This information is elicited only through well-written and in-depth features on issues which are of direct relevance to the people.
(iv) Increasing number of women-journalists in the profession and the growing recognition of the role of women in society has spawned features on a number of issues concerning gender, children and women, family, health and nutrition, and other societal concerns. These features find a wide readership across the spectrum.
(v) A number of newspapers have added regular theme pages on different subjects—technology, gadgets, agriculture, health, education, careers, travel, science, investment and several

others. Features naturally form a major segment of these theme pages.

(vi) News magazines and week-end supplements have created a continuously growing market for feature writers. Newspapers are facing a serious competition on several fronts. Since magazines are becoming more innovative and offer more value for money, newspapers have to redesign their style contents and presentation. Features offer the newspapers sufficient scope for this type of adaptation.

(vii) Good features enable the readers to convert information into understanding and develop proper appreciation of the issues involved. Good features constitute good journalism, which enhances the overall standards in the industry. According to Val Williams, Editing Consultant with the Thomson Foundation, features can work in several ways. Features can:

- Explain what is happening;
- Expand on a news item, an official statement;
- Explore ideas, new concepts;
- Investigate issues, social problems, scandals;
- Describe events large and small, places, experiences, journeys, people;
- Entertain with humour, perhaps, or colourful description;
- Campaign for the righting of wrongs, the improvement of the human condition; and
- Comment usually in the form of column.

There are no hard and fast rules for feature writing. A young journalist who wants to develop feature writing should read as many features as possible in both Indian and foreign magazines. With the advent of social media and websites, the task of reading foreign magazines has become easy. Gone are the days when writers, journalists and bookworms used to throng the libraries of embassies and foreign consulates.

Just as there are no rules for feature writing, there are also no limits to what subjects can make a feature. A feature can be narrative, descriptive or expository. It used to be said that a good feature writer could be parachuted on to the North Pole and even in that bleak wasteland produce a good feature. A feature is a product of the heart. Its subject matter is specific, even narrow. It is based on feelings and personal reactions of the writer to people, places and happenings. The purpose of a feature is to provide information, education and entertainment. Photographs and illustrations are essential accompaniments in a feature.

Types of Features

There are various kinds of features, depending on the subject, time and theme. These can be profile features, news features, photo-features, human interest features, those on development issues and on travel and hospitality. We discuss these in detail.

I. Profiles: A personality profile is written to bring a reader close to an eminent personality who may be in or out of news. Interviews with or about a leading person—observations, anecdotes, significant happenings, personality traits, failings and foibles, details from the living contemporaries of the late personality, add colour to the narrative. People enjoy reading about other people, which makes a personality profile a popular feature. Every year we come across a large number of features on Mahatma Gandhi, John Kennedy, Martin Luther King and other personalities, highlighting different aspects of their lives they lived and the philosophy they propounded. The stories of eminent men and women are worth telling even several years after they have gone. Human interest in them survives long after they are dead. Features can be written on their lives and works, their achievements and contribution to the nation. These features continue to be of interest to the readers.

Scores of feature articles on Amartya Sen appeared after the well-known economist won the Nobel Prize. The way Amartya Sen had been catapulted to the status of a folk hero in Shantiniketan, the rejoicing, the excitement, his school days, recollections and reminiscences of his friends and teachers—all aspects were recounted in numerous interviews taken with his mother. Here is an excerpt from *Outlook* of 26 October, 1998.

> *In her sun washed verandah crammed with memories, a proud mother picks up the phone, and dials New York in room full of*

people. "Can you put me through to Amartya Sen please, who got the Nobel Prize. I am his mother speaking." When a sleepy Sen comes on the line, there is a torrent of motherly advice: return to Cambridge carefully, eat properly, and take rest. "They are coming in droves here, Amartya," she says. "India is proud of you, but Shantiniketan is agog with excitement." When the scholar comes visiting again this winter, Shantiniketan will fete its proudest son—after Tagore.

The profile features written by senior journalist Harihar Swarup in *The Sunday Tribune* every week covers a wide spectrum of public figures—politicians, diplomats, artists and others currently in news. The profile of the forest brigand titled as the Lord of the Jungle in *The Tribune*, 16 December, 2002 narrates in detail Veerappan's crime record, his strategy of survival and important traits of his character. The gripping account of his crimes—130 murders, sandalwood smuggling running into crores of rupees, and his ruthlessness makes an interesting reading.

It is not that profiles of only eminent philosophers, great leaders, thinkers and social reformers are read with interest; the profiles of social climbers, street smart persons who cut corners to become rich and influential, arm dealers and even crooks make equally, if not more, engrossing features.

II. News Features: A news feature represents an opportunity to look into greater detail at a story currently in news, where deadlines and space allowed room for little more than the bare facts.

A news feature could be an in-depth story, through extensive research and interviews and provides details well beyond a basic news story or a feature. A lengthy news feature may examine one topic extensively.

In his book on *Advanced Reporting*, Bruce Garrison says: News features are news stories that take a feature approach. They are features that appear in the traditional news portions of a newspaper or a magazine. News feature reporters often look for a story about someone or something not usually a newsmaker.

III. Photo Features/Photo Essays: Journalism is undergoing a visual revolution. Photo features and photo essays in magazines and even Sunday newspapers have contributed to making the media scene bright and colourful. Illustrations have become indispensable. A good editor always looks forward to quality photographs and infographics to give life to happenings and people in newspapers and magazines. A media academic notes: Newspaper pages that were grey columns of type broken by black and white photographs have been transformed into well-designed packages integrating words, photographs, illustrations and graphics.

The magazine revolution has, in fact, also heralded the visual revolution. Magazines have been long known for their innovative designing and photographs. *Life* has been one such magazine of its type. *The Illustrated Weekly of India* used to have news in pictures, photographs and pictorial features. Photojournalists are considered equal partners with journalists. Events and happenings are being recorded on video and photographs through digital cameras. Historic events across the world are captured through camera in a way that their memory lingers long after the events are over.

The on-the-spot report about the break-up of the Soviet Union—End of an Empire—in the *India Today* issue of 15 September, 1991, with the cover depicting the kicking of the toppled statue of the founder of KGB, Felix Dzherzhinsky, succeeded in giving the readers a blow-by-blow account of the events convulsing the country. The features, profusely illustrated with graphics and colour photographs, made the readers feel that they were witnessing the events first hand. This is an example of a true sign of good journalism. Let us look at some photo features and photo essays:

(1) Still Life in a Mobile World, *Outlook*, 27 December, 1999: An unusual photo feature on millions of statues littered throughout the country's streetscape and how these are maintained. For instance, Gandhiji's statue near Suraj Kund in Haryana was found convenient for smoking; Nehru's statue in Bhopal was plastered with posters. The statues have become standardized items of the streetscape like government-approved items in offices—desks, chairs, paperweights. Equally interesting was as to how making of statues was ordered through lowest tender for each part; facial features, eyes etc. A truly bizarre procedure for a work of art.

(2) Iraq: Lost World, *India Today*, 4 November, 2002: More than half a dozen photographs of all sizes depict the life of Saddam Hussein's country of 25 million—a human drama depicting every possible emotion. Iraq, which was once throbbing with life and activity, now just tired. Some unusual photographs of people queuing for scarce water in a country where oil is in plenty, a couple celebrating their wedding and several others.

(3) The Wounds of Salt, *India Today*, 17 March, 2008: This photo essay shows the harsh working conditions of a little-known tribe of Gujarat which produces most of the country's salt. The Agarias, or salt pan workers, live a life of poverty, serve under a cycle of debt and battle tough working conditions every single day. The nature of work is such that the men are heavily into liquor and tobacco. The result is that a high percentage of these men die young. Even though entire families work together, they still cannot make a profit. Exploitation by middlemen and traders ensures that they live in the most primitive conditions. The photographs depict the work, the stark landscape and the poverty of the people.

(4) Rebuilding Nepal's Heritage, *Mint*, 15 July, 2016: This photo essay shows how after the devastating earthquakes, Nepal is trying to rebuild and restore its priceless heritage and architecture. The earthquakes in 2015 had severely damaged the Kathmandu valley and many other districts in Nepal, taking the lives of thousands of people and rendering lakhs homeless. Also damaged were scores of World Heritage Monuments leading to a considerable loss of revenue from tourism. The photographs show how experts are working with local crafts persons to restore the heritage structures and how many temples have been supported with stilts.

IV. Human Interest Features: Human interest features generally focus on an individual rather than a group, the actual subject or event is related to a feeling or an emotion. These stories have colour, humour, description, anecdotes, drama and emotion. Many human interest stories focus on an odd or unusual event. These features discuss human aspects or human problems rather than higher human values or philosophical aspects of human existence.

One good tip which an aspiring feature writer would do well to remember is that readers are more interested in people than they are in things. Therefore, features, even if they are about things have to be written around people doing the things or affected by things. Human interest stories are written to show a subject's oddity or its practical, emotional or entertainment value. These stories discuss matters or events that are of basic interest or concern to the people. If such stories are light and humorous, they may be called page brighteners. Let us look at two stories, which can be considered as human interest features:

(1) Sajjo, *Hindustan Times*, 23 June, 2000

Chained to a block of wood that weighs nearly 20 kg, 12-year-old Sajjo spends her days in the shadow of social stigma. Bruises and deep gashes are common on her fragile form. Sajjo's fault? She is mentally challenged and described as a 'terror' by residents of Kali Kalyanpura. Sajjo hits children, steals food and goods from shops. Her parents said she slipped out of the house one day.

Neighbours told Sajjo's mother, Sayra, that she was seen boarding a bus.

"Finally, she was brought back by some people. They had seen her sing and dance and passengers rewarded her by throwing coins," recalled Sayra.

The incident spread around in Turkman Gate and she was branded as 'pagal'. People started throwing stones at her and would beat her up without provocation. Sajjo's parents were forced to chain her.

The photograph accompanying the story shows a young girl with short-cropped hair and wearing a blue salwar tunic. She could be any Indian teenager. The story further gives details of her family and her parents and makes out that Sajjo was not a '*pagal*'. Only if her parents could afford to send her to a hospital.

(2) Student Who Turns Street Food Vendor by Night, *Indian Express*, 20 February, 2016

Eighteen-year-old Madhav Mishra reckons the street food joint he runs at a junction on Linking Road in Khar is the most underrated. There are no fancy chairs or tables. Nor does it have a roof. But Mishra's eatery on Harnam Singh Chadda Chowk starts filling up after 11 every night as he caters to at least 120 customers. They range from guards or watchmen at buildings close by, restaurant delivery boys and auto-rickshaw drivers.

Setting up shop daily isn't much of a chore. Madhav has limited props for the night—three large buckets and two medium ones, each of which comprises some home cooked Indian cuisine; a few five-litre water containers and 200 thermocol plates.

"Nearly two years ago, my uncle, a rickshaw driver in the city, suggested the idea of starting something to cater to rickshaw drivers who work late night," Madhav recalled. The youth lives with his mother and sister in a slum in Khar Danda area and moved to Mumbai in 2011.

This is an interesting story that profiles a student who dreams of becoming an engineer one day. A migrant from Bihar to Mumbai, he helps his mother run the household by selling food to guards, rickshaw pullers and other labourers at night.

V. Features on Environment: As environmental problems take a toll on the society, more and more scientists, media persons, environmentalists and citizens fear that the ability of our natural systems to sustain themselves will collapse. In this regard, the mass-media plays a strategic role in promoting public awareness and shaking its attitude in favour of sustainable development. The media also push the governments into doing more to bring environment-friendly policies and protecting the environment.

Environmental issues are diverse, ranging from local issues to global problems—therefore, can be complex and a journalist has to develop understanding before he can write about them effectively and with conviction. Not all environmental reporting may turn out to be breaking news as a large part of environment writing remains in the domain of features. For instance, if you have to write a feature about how an area is losing vegetation because of over-population, you would benefit from background knowledge about the population issue, government policies, economic, social and cultural practices that could contribute to the loss of vegetation, biological and weather conditions in the region. This background would also help you to identify good sources for interviews in governmental and non-governmental bodies and universities.

The lines that separate feature, interpretive and investigative reporting are not sharply delineated. Frequently you will find elements of both interpretive and investigative reporting in feature articles, particularly those that try to examine and provide perspective on complex and controversial issues. Conversely, an interpretive or investigative article could take a feature, rather than hard news approach for presenting information to readers.

The Illustrated Weekly of India, in its issue named: *Whose life is it anyway? Does anyone care for the victims of the world's worst industrial catastrophe?* dated 30 December, 1984-January 1985, devoted several features to the aftermath of the Bhopal Gas Tragedy. Various dimensions of the event—environmental hazards, industrial safety, industrialization and ethical aspects were discussed in detail. Many writers and reporters had put in a lot of research into writing the varied pieces and numerous story ideas related to the disaster and its lasting impact on the sufferings of the people.

Mint, in its article *Millennials who are saving the planet one cause, one species at a time*, dated 8 October, 2018, has featured three young environmentalists making serious efforts to preserve environment and protect species. The feature profiles three professionals from Delhi and Bengaluru who have taken up different routes to work on conservation and environment. They are doing their bit for environment through court cases, research and policy as well as photography and story-telling so that it becomes interesting for children to understand species, ecology and the need to safeguard our ecology. It is a simple interview-based feature in which the writer has spoken to three young and passionate people working to protect environment.

VI. Features on Travel and Tourism: Travel and tourism offers scope for writing interesting features with good quality photographs on a wide variety of subjects—tourist destinations, places of pilgrimage, wild life sanctuaries, food and cuisines and several others. Of late, there has been an upsurge in the number of features and articles appearing on travel and tourism. Writing on travel and tourism has become fashionable also because of the plethora of niche magazines catering exclusively to travel and holidays. Even in-flight magazines of airlines, for instance, *Swagat* of the Indian Airlines and even the *Rail Neer* of the Indian Railways have led this boom in travel and tourism writing.

Let us look at the two features published in these magazines:

Swagat of October 1998 in the travel feature—*Going with the Ganga*—third Ganga Water Rally from Allahabad to Varanasi gives an engrossing account of Sangam, Sadhus and Ghats. The article is about adventure tourism and seeks to showcase the architectural and historical banks of the river. The opening of this feature is quite evocative. "Men got their heads tonsured. Bathers offered morning prayers to the sun. Flocks of ducks disturbed by the drone of our boat flapped their wings and took to the air. We were almost at the Sangam. You can make out the two rivers by the colour of their waters—the Ganga appears muddy, while the Yamuna is blue."

Let us look at another travel article. *Outlook Traveller* of August 3, 2018, in the feature, *Discover Imphal's Food Culture in These Eateries*, where, as the title itself suggests, the writer has made food the focus of a tourist's attention. The article highlights some of the top restaurants in Imphal, the capital of Manipur, in North East India where tourists can savour authentic local cuisine. The writer also narrates some of the important historical highlights like the Battle of Imphal during World War II to the elusive sangai deer. However, the focus remains on Manipuri cuisine, for which the author has singled out six good places to eat in the city.

Tips for Writing Features

So far we have discussed some of the important aspects of feature writing—definitions, importance of features, different types of features and related examples. In the examples above, you will notice that there is no single way to writing a feature unlike the case with news—which is rigid and strictly follows 'Five Ws and One H'. However, the following tips will help you organize yourself for writing features:

(i) Whatever your topic, find out people who are experts and can give you indepth knowledge. Also, find out what has been published on the subject before.

(ii) Feature writing begins with an idea. Ideas come from reading—newspapers, magazines, books, reports, studies conducted by research institutes and NGOs. Keep writing these ideas from time to time so that you can develop these into features later.

(iii) Listen to what people are talking about. Sometimes, good feature ideas are to be found right under your nose—conversations on the bus, problems citizens face at the local municipal office and specially watch out for trends and lifestyle changes. Any subject, with a little effort and imagination, can yield good feature.

(iv) News stories can offer great ideas for feature articles. Develop the idea further so that what has not been reported in news can be developed into a feature story.

(v) Your features should synchronise with definite occasions—aniversaries and events. For instance, a feature on harmful effects of smoking will find more acceptance on the anti-tobacco day organized by WHO.

(vi) And do not be afraid of Blank Sheet Syndrome. Every writer faces it. Sometimes, the idea to start writing a story is just not there. The very first sentence is proving to be evasive. So, the best way to overcome this phenomenon is to give yourself a little break, take a walk, do some chore and come back with a fresher and less anxious mind.

REFERENCES

Friedrich Ebert Stiftung, *The Newsroom*, Bonn (Germany).

Gupta, V.S. and Indu Grover (1996): Study Material, for the participants in, Refresher Course on Communication Skills and Reporting, Haryana Agricultural University.

Sethi, Patanjali (1974): *Professional Journalism*, Orient Longman.

Singh, S. Nihal (1992): *Your Slip is Showing*, Indian Press Today, UBS Publishers Distributors, New Delhi.

8

Development Reporting

Highlighting the Human Dimension

The concept of development journalism is not new, although the term itself came into common journalistic usage only during the early sixties. Like so many labels, its definitions can be stretched to embrace a number of subjects and issues. Development journalism could be dull and boring. However, well done, it is readable and informative. It could also be educative and inspirational, particularly the innovative experiments and success stories being undertaken to improve the human conditions throughout the country, specially in small towns and villages.

Definition

"Development journalism seeks to report a country's progress and setbacks in both urban and rural areas in a factual and readable way. It should create an information bridge between the authorities and the public, between urban and rural communities. Long term, it aims to contribute to improvements in people's lifestyles."

The training kit, prepared by the Thomson Foundation/UNICEF for Human Development Reporting, discusses development reporting in terms of PEOPLE. The emphasis in such examples is on people because it is after all the people who are building the nation. If development means anything, it must mean development of a better framework of existence for the people—the men, women and the children. An effective news organization should record their progress.

It must give them information which will enable them to improve their productive capacity. It must show them how to improve their bargaining power with society.

CNN's former South Asia Bureau Chief, Anita Pratap, defines development journalism as *"reporting on issues such as population, healthcare, illiteracy, poverty and environment..."* (*Outlook*, 18 January, 1999).

Here it will be in order to discuss very briefly as to what development stands for. It stands for removal of poverty, lessening of poverty between regions, classes and different sections of society, building up to technological infrastructure and modernization of society through education. It is measured in terms of the improvement in the lives of the people.

One of the most inspiring books on the subject—*India 2020: A Vision for the New Millennium*—is devoted to projecting an action plan whereby India can reach a developed country status by 2020. It spells out what a developed status means as under:

> *"What does the developed nation status mean in terms of the common man? It means the major transformation of our national economy to make it one of the largest economies in the world; where the countrymen live well above the poverty line, their education and health is of high standard; national security reasonably assured, and the core competence in certain major areas gets enhanced significantly so that the production of quality goods, including exports, is rising and thereby bringing all-round prosperity for the countrymen. What is the common link needed to realize these sub-goals? It is the technological strength of the nation, which is the key to reach this developed status."*

Positive Media

Media can make a significant contribution towards directing the energies and capabilities of the people towards realization of this vision. In this context the authors say:

> *"The media plays an important role in any modern society in*

> *moulding public opinion. It has its own constraints. Like any enterprise, it has to make a profit. The media presents news, views and analyses tailored to suit what the readers would like. It also has to create headlines, look for something shocking, exciting or thrilling. But Pokhran, or an Indian victory in a cricket match, or some other positive event does not occur everyday. Generally, the focus is on the negative: a gory event, on worrying developments. Such coverage has gone to a point that a situation much more worse than actually the case is being presented.*
>
> *We do not at all believe that the press' role is not to criticize and not to highlight problems. There is also at times a need to exaggerate events to make a point. But we feel too that it is time now that the media attempts a more positive outlook, reporting at least one positive event a day ! Devote a part of the paper to say something good about India which is real and not false. If the major papers do this, there will be a great attitudinal change in the country. Similarly, the electronic media can also help create a new climate: report one good event a day not just from a metropolis or city but from different parts of the country.*

So what stories should the development reporter cover? They breakdown into two very broad categories:

Project-related: Projects can range from building a new hydro-electric power station to water harvesting projects in a village that has scarcity of water, from devising new methods of adult and informal education to devising a new crop-rotation system in agriculture.

Issue-related: Issues are even more varied. These issues usually are about problems that have to be solved—and also about how the solution has been found in a few cases. Exploitation of women as cheap labour, on the one hand, and formation of a women's co-operative society for giving them credit are several such issues on which informative and interesting features can be written. Some other issues could be: What happens when the overwhelming pressure on families to produce sons rather than daughters has led to an imbalance in the sexes—the problem which is becoming quite acute in states like Haryana and

Punjab. Subjects such as health, education, employment, empowerment and elimination of poverty call for sustained and regular coverage as a part of development reporting.

The basic purpose of development journalism, as with other forms of journalism, is to inform, educate and entertain. Since people need basic information about the development programmes and plans envisaged by various departments of the government, information should be presented in an interesting and intelligible manner so that the intended beneficiaries are fully aware of all aspects. Equally important function of development journalism is to investigate, analyse and interpret such plans. In the past, development journalism has been criticized for its tendency to depend wholly on government organizations, media officers and others who, in the name of development news, tried to make propaganda even about those programmes which were not really useful for the people.

Development news is not PR handout, which presents list of success stories achieved by governments in different areas. In a country like India, where even after 55 years of independence, there are visible pockets of poverty and distress, there would always be need for in-depth study and analysis of the failures as well as successes. Development journalism should seek to create an enabling environment, which through increased and accurate information facilitates the development process itself. It makes the expert knowledge available where it is needed and provides an opportunity for exchange of views and discussion.

The contemporary media is becoming more and more market-oriented. Embracing the spirit of consumerism, the news media has moved away from reporting substantive happenings in villages and small towns. In an interesting and detailed coverage of the ongoings in the media, the *Gentleman* magazine, in its issue of June 1999, carried an incisive article by the Director of the Press Institute of India, Ajit Bhattacharjea, who lamented the lack of balance in media coverage, specifically the limited coverage given to the grassroots India. However, with a sprinkling of committed journalists, we keep getting news and features that objectively report on the human condition. We shall discuss some of these noteworthy initiatives in development reporting with a view to highlighting the important contribution that this type of reporting can make to the nation-building process.

Noteworthy Initiatives on Development Reporting

Everybody Loves a Good Drought: Stories from India's Poorest Districts: This book by P. Sainath, gives a graphic account of rampant corruption prevailing at the grassroots level of development bureaucracy. He reported about destruction of traditional irrigation systems and development schemes, which had done more harm than good, role of money lenders and failure of land reforms. Sainath, however, could see a new mood among the poor who had started understanding about the way the plans were being implemented and the corruption involved in implementation. He wrote, "In different parts of the country, people are asserting themselves against great odds in different ways. In some cases, these may not be the healthiest of ways. But all of them represent this reality, the ruled are no longer willing to be ruled in the old way."

Grassroots—Reporting the Human Condition: Published monthly, Grassroots looks at a range of social and development issues from across the country. The publication looks at environment, conditions in rural areas, change-makers and government schemes. A lot of the stories that are written from rural areas put the spotlight on women achievers and their struggles. The first issue of the journal appeared in May 1999 with the initiative taken up by Bhattacharjea to bring about a balance in media coverage of grassroots India. At that time he had said that "we find nothing in the papers about panchayats, and empowerment, agriculture and the rural economy, literacy, unemployment, social tension. Yet without such coverage, the press fails its democratic function of monitoring the condition of society as a whole. It cannot claim the status of the Fourth Estate." Twenty years later, Grassroots still covers the vital engines of empowerment like Panchayati Raj, literacy, rural economy, unemployment, water and power issues showing the possibilities and range of topics which form the core of development reporting.

***The Water Harvesters—A Chapter from Mark Tully's book,* India in Slow Motion:** By no means a part of development reporting, the chapter goes on to show as to how development topics like working of panchayats, agriculture, drought are attracting the attention of media.

In this book, which covers a diverse range of subjects—from child labour, sufi mysticism to the crisis in agriculture, a chapter on water harvesting by the farmers in Gujarat, one of the drought stricken states, makes fascinating reading. Here Tully explains the efforts of the village people of Rajsandhiyala in constructing small dams holding water in previously dried-up rivulets, and the ponds which collected and allowed to percolate through the soil to raise the ground water level. These are classified as 'minor irrigation works' as against the major dams and canals.

Tully saw check dams during his visit to several villages in Saurashtra, where Narmada dam was considered to be the only answer to the region's problems. He concludes his chapter while endorsing the observations of the sarpanch of village Rajsandhiyala: "I do not see why we should not have both—water harvesting and Narmada. Certainly if we have Narmada, that does not mean we should waste water."

Mark Tully points out in his book, "Civil society is vibrant, India has become the NGO capital of the world. Television has grown from a drab purveyor of government propaganda to a multichannel independent media. The press, once obsessed with politics, now provides news and bewildering variety of views on every aspect of Indian life, including the misdeeds of those who wield power." Development reporting offers precisely such an opportunity to the journalists who wish to report from the farms and the fields.

Finding Story Ideas

Observe and think: Development story ideas, both positive and negative in nature, are all-around us. Just by careful observation during your travels you might turn up with development issues of interest to people.

Government reports: Reports by various ministries and the Planning Commission constitute a rich source of information for development issues. Frequently, a reporter can sift stories out of government reports as these are full of important information and statistics which provide excellent leads for stories. The same holds true for making sources in the government as government officials might quietly give hints of a story or leak information in public interest.

International organizations: These are good sources for feature stories as they bring before journalists the latest development thinking and research happening in international fora. The publications issued by various UN agencies like WHO, FAO, WHO and UNEP also provide an international perspective from which to evaluate the actions of our own government.

NGOs: Local NGOs that are working with the people and communities on various development issues are a good source of stories. These organisations work on health, education, child rights, labour, environment and other grassroots concerns thereby becoming a rich source of story ideas from the grassroots.

Universities: A good source of development story ideas are research organisations and universities. As scientists do wide ranging research and studies in biology, ecology, air pollution, geology, agriculture, forestry, hydrology, and several other subjects they are a repository of ideas for new articles.

Constraints in Development Reporting

The Indian press—by far the freest press in South Asia, pluralistic, multilingual, continues to be largely urban oriented. More so the newspapers coming out from the national capital which are Delhi-centric. The press in English language is elitist, geared to commercial culture, obsessed with garnering the maximum share of advertising revenue. Development issues are not given adequate coverage. Reporting development issues is constrained by several factors. According to popular perceptions, development reporting is not considered glamorous or prestigious enough in the reporter's scale of prestige. Development reporting occupies a low rung. Every young reporter dreams of covering politics, defence or foreign policy, rather than specialising in development reporting.

Another reason is that a lot of the reporters have urban backgrounds and they hardly understand the rural milieu or how communities live at the grassroots. They find it difficult to understand agricultural policies, co-operative societies, the role of caste, village politics and the complex agrarian economy.

Dos and Don'ts in Development Reporting

(i) Development reporting must describe the people at work in the projects and processes. It must describe the processes of change and modernization, the innovations and improvements. The reporter must not use phrases directly from official communications.

(ii) A reporter writing on development issues must develop an outlook that is sympathetic to the cause of the people who are the subjects of his reporting.

(iii) A development journalist should acquire basic understanding of terms used in agriculture, environment, science, urban planning and economic development. While reporting on tribal or 'hill-areas', it is necessary to understand the customs and traditions of the people of that area.

(iv) Even though you may be dealing with technical subjects, do not bring them into your writing. If you must use a technical term, define it as soon as possible, after you use it. Never use the stiff, formal writing style of science and technology reports.

(v) A development journalist must maintain regular contacts with a wide range of persons and organizations—NGOs, CSOs, VOs, universities and research institutions. International organizations like WHO, UNICEF, UNDP publish useful reports on a number of subjects. Human Development Reports published by UNDP and the World Bank Reports are particularly precious source of information and help a writer build proper perspective.

(vi) Read what well-known development journalists like Bharat Dogra and P. Sainath have been writing. Their writings could suggest you many leads and clues on the subjects you could write on.

And finally development reporting is more a state of mind than technique of reporting. If you develop that state of mind, it may be only a matter of time before success comes your way.

REFERENCES

Bhattacharjea, Ajit (1999-2002): *Grassroots*, Various Issues, Press Institute of India, New Delhi.

Gupta, V.S. (2000): *Communication and Development: The Challenge of the Twenty First Century*, Concept Publishing Company, New Delhi.

Gupta, V.S. (2003): *Communication, Development and Civil Society*, Concept Publishing Company Pvt. Ltd., New Delhi.

Kalam, APJ Abdul with Y.S. Rajan (1998): *India 2020: A Vision for the New Millennium*, Penguin Books, New Delhi.

Mark Tully & Gillian Wright (2002): *India in Slow Motion*, Penguin Books, New Delhi.

Sainath, P. (1996): *Everybody Loves a Good Drought—Stories from India's Poorest Districts*, Penguin Books, New Delhi.

The Thomson Foundation/UNICEF (1994), *Children & Women in the News*, Cardiff, United Kingdom.

9

Editing

The Final Gatekeeping Process

Editing is an art and a technique, which involves a number of activities: revising, amending, checking, correcting, polishing, rephrasing, rewriting. It also means putting together, rearranging, reordering and selecting the material to be finally published.

Editing may also be defined as: Correcting and adapting the text of an article, news story or a book so as to make it suitable for publishing:

- Collecting several pieces of writing by different authors and preparing them for publishing.
- An edit is defined by the Cobuild English Dictionary as a process of examining and correcting a text so that it is suitable for publishing.

Editing is the work of a team of skilled persons who, while working in a newspaper, can scan the vast see of words, make a selection, cut down what is selected to size and serve it up attractively to its readers. There has to be selection because, irrespective of the size of the paper, the amount of material that a newspaper gets is much more than it has the space to print.

All this process of reporting, checking, correcting, rephrasing and rewriting, and the final selection of the material used in the newspaper is undertaken by a team of reporters, sub-editors, chief-subs and news editor under the leadership of the editor.

We have already discussed several aspects of this process in different chapters. Here we shall discuss techniques and principles of editing, proof reading, designing and layout of the pages, and other important features, so that the written material is made fit for publishing in a style generally acceptable to the readers.

Principles of Editing

Editing includes sub-editing or, in short, subbing. In a newspaper a sub-editor handles the reporter's copy, , press releases and all types of news that flows in. He checks facts and figures, spellings and grammar, names and identification etc. If need be he may rewrite the news story in order to give it a proper news angle, he may also condense the report more effectively and improve the language.

No amount of theorizing about the principles and techniques of editing will help you without hands-on practice. The effort will be futile, just like trying to learn swimming without getting wet. However, some basic principles of editing, based on author's experience and collected from different sources are given below for your understanding and guidance.

1. Paying Attention to Language: The foremost principle is to make the copy readable. The sub-editor/editor must ensure that the story conforms to the following five principles:

(i) It is precise.
(ii) It is clear.
(iii) It has a pace appropriate to the content.
(iv) It uses transitional devices that lead the reader from one thought to the next.
(v) It appeals to the reader's senses.

Writing is precise when words are used in the way they should be used. It is clear when simple sentences and correct grammar are employed. A long sentence makes tedious reading and slows the reader. Sharp, descriptive words appeal to the reader's senses to bring him or her close to action.

A newsman's language is the people's language, the language in which the public thinks, the public talks and the public understands. Ordinary men must understand every word. A newspaper language is meant not for scholars, but the laypersons and it should, therefore, cater to their sensibilities and requirement. An editor has to keep in mind the following points for writing a story:

- Use short simple words.
- Use familiar words.
- Use personal words.
- Make every word work.
- Avoid technical words.
- Do your cutting in such a way as to preserve the essential facts, leaving just enough detail to answer the readers most pressing questions.
- Get rid of rubber stamp phrases.
- Use intimate phrases.
- Make short, simple paragraphs.
- Write for a specific purpose.
- Write with one viewpoint.
- Try to preserve the flavour of the story when it is built around a feature.
- Remove excess wordage at any stage.

(Examples of rubber stamp phrases/redundant words and their correct forms are given in the Appendix-I at the end of the chapter.)

2. Rewriting: Rewriting a news story is equally essential to ensure that the headline accurately reflects the news captured in the text, and the focus of the story is not lost in the "wordiness." The one book which the present author keeps on going back to, again and again, is *Write for Success*, by Gregory A. Barnes. Barnes underlines the importance of rewriting in one memorable sentence: "Rewriting usually makes the difference between the mediocre and good paper". Even while in a hurry to catch the deadline, a good sub-editor would not ignore rewriting aspect of editing. Use of proper words is another important principle of editing. It will be worthwhile to inculcate the practice of using proper words while writing news stories, features and reports.

3. Inverted Pyramid Model of Writing News: The writing of news follows a certain pattern. The most interesting part of the event, the most unusual, the most striking facts, or the facts which are the most rewarding to the reader or the 'climax' of the story, come first. The remaining facts are presented in the body in the descending order of importance. This is called the Inverted Pyramid model of writing. In this model, the lead as the summary of the most important facts forms the base. At the top, there are important details in one or two paragraphs, followed by more details and additional facts supporting the main news. Minor details and the less important facts constitute the bottom.

The advantage of writing news in this form is that the lead is able to catch the reader's interest. It enables him to decide whether it will be good for him to go through the rest of the story. Being in hurry, if the reader does not read the story beyond the lead; he still catches the essential points of the news. This is also of advantage to the editor. If he does not have enough space for printing the whole of your news story he will be able to cut down its length by removing the latter paragraphs, without losing any of the essential facts of the story. This model of news writing has been explained earlier in the second chapter.

4. Deciding About the Lead: The news lead is similar to the first few sentences with which you begin telling your friends the outcome of some meeting or to your family member about an event which you have witnessed. It is important to note that the news begins with date line which gives the name of the place where the event took place and the date on which it happened or is reported.

Layout and Design

Layout

Designing, make up and layout of a newspaper are paid as much attention as the editorial. Packaging and presentation of a paper, photographs, graphics and production are important considerations.

About the significance of layout, T.J.S. George says:

(i) The first thing to understand is the purpose of layout. There is no dispute about this: the sole objective of layout is to help the reader locate and peruse the day's news with absolute ease.

(ii) Secondly, the sub-editor should know what are the elements at his disposal to achieve the layout he wants. Here too there is no debate: the elements that go into the make-up of a page are the headlines, blocs of body matter, pictures and other graphics, column rules and/or white space, and a fixed component in the shape of the day's advertising quantum on the given page.

(iii) Thirdly, he must know how to use the elements he has to reach the make-up goal he sets himself.

This is where expertise comes into play and the ability to choose wisely among contending schools of thought.

The basic principle of newspaper design, apart from making the product an attractive, saleable proposition, is to give the paper an identity, what kind of newspaper is to be produced and what kind of readership it is catering to.

A newspaper must look like a newspaper and not like a train timetable or poster advertising a football match. A properly designed newspaper will aim to draw the reader's eye from one part of the page to another in an orderly and intelligent system. Readers should not expect to battle their way through a maze of written wordage. The basic rule for newspaper design should really be the same as the basic rule in all other aspects of journalism—clarity and simplicity.

Design—Smart Look and Sleek Size

Designing has become one of the most significant factors in contemporary journalism. Newspapers and magazines are taking to unconventional and innovative designing. With the on-set of computerized publishing, the system of layout and designing the page has completely changed. The newspapers have taken to smart look and sleek size.

Picture Editing

The value of a photograph as a means of communication has been long accepted in communication and journalism circles. A photograph needs no words—except perhaps for a brief caption. Even a person with little education can understand a picture. Research has shown that most newspaper readers recall more easily the main news picture than the most widely read news story of that day.

It is not only the photographs but any illustration—diagram, map, cartoon or line drawing—which can be an important communication tool. A newspaper photographer has long been recognized as a journalist in his own right. He must be skilled not only in the handling of a camera; he needs the insight and experience to be at the right place at the right time—to 'get the story' through his camera. A news photographer, in addition to the pictures, also provides a caption giving details of the subject matter.

In editing photographs, the aim should be to increase the visual impact. Just as a skilful sub-editor may brighten a dull piece of writing, imaginative editing can transform a disappointing print into an interesting picture.

A picture must be judged not only on its technical excellence—bright, sharp, well composed, but also on its news value. The newsworthiness, and whether it conforms to accepted standards of honest reporting and good taste, should be the main consideration in evaluating the relevance of a picture.

Headlines

Every morning, when a reader looks for something interesting in a newspaper, it is the headline which catches his eyes. After scanning the headings, he settles down to read the story in detail. A story, howsoever well-edited, would not attract him unless it is given a heading or headline which is eye-catching. The headline tempts the reader to go through the story. It tells him what the story is about. Thus, a headline sells the story. The size of the headline determines the importance of a story: the larger or bolder the headline, the more important is the news story.

A distinguished Indian editor once took a week off from his office and did nothing but watch people buying newspapers from the street. He followed them into buses or restaurants to watch how they were reading the paper. Even allowing for the fact that some of the people who bought the paper would have taken it home and perhaps given it a more thorough examination there, the editor made important discoveries during his week away from the office. He found that the great majority of readers rarely spent more than a few minutes looking at the newspaper and only a few stories were read from the beginning to the end. For most part, the readers glanced over the pages and only if something caught their eye did they read on. Obviously, the first thing that caught their eye were the headlines to the stories.

Writing a headline is like applying the finishing polish on a well-crafted piece of furniture. While writing headlines, you should keep the following points in mind:

(i) A headline should speak. It should say something which educates and entertains the reader.
(ii) A headline should stimulate the reader and lead him to reading the story under it. A news item with a bad headline does not get read.
(iii) A headline should be sharp and convey the essence of a story.
(iv) A headline should be active and positive. The best headline is written in the present tense, because it provides a sense of immediacy.

Headlines are a line or collection of lines of display type that precede a story and introduces it. Headlines are sentences, built around action verbs. They must be adjusted to a pre-determined space and typographical style.

Headlines

(i) Convey the reader the relative significance of the news by the type display.
(ii) Give the readers an idea of what the stories contain.
(iii) Provide variety in the newspaper, design and make pages attractive.

The headline should be simple, easy to understand, informative, should be capable of being read quickly and proportionate to the news.

The headlines:

- Must carry an active verb.
- Should be in the present tense.
- Avoid abbreviations.
- Comma can be used in place of and.

Intro

The intro to a song, programme or a book is the first part, which comes before the main part. The facts that should go in the first sentence of the news is also called the intro. If the intro to a story is not clear, straightforward and interesting then the whole purpose of writing the story is lost. In case the first sentence of the story is not clear to the readers, and does not hold their interest because it is not interesting, then the readers will prefer to skip the story.

The intro should consist of one smoothly flowing sentence of not more than about 25 words. Very rarely will it contain more than two sentences. The second of which is in the immediate context of the first. The intro should seize upon the news point—that is, the most interesting thing of the story. The sound rule of intro is that it should answer the questions: Who? Why? What? Where? When? However, in case of such an intro, it may include too many facts, thus losing focus of the story.

Book Reviews

The book review column is considered a popular column by scholars, librarians, publishers and all others interested in keeping themselves informed of the latest arrivals. Book reviews are done by editorial staff of the newspapers and subject matter specialists. Whereas most of the book reviews are quite informative and add to reader's knowledge, sometimes the reviewers write reviews either to settle personal scores (the reviewer and the author whose book is being reviewed being rivals in the same profession) or flaunt mastery over the subject. Both are fatal flaws in a reviewer.

As a matter of ethics, a reviewer should be an impartial judge of the contents of the book under review. He should not impose his prejudices on the readers. There are instances where a senior teacher of journalism, who reviews books on the subject, starting a campaign against another eminent scholar—commenting more about the latter's contribution to the discipline, rather than on the book itself. He has also been running down his colleagues, from the same institution, while reviewing their books. That amounts to misusing the privilege as a reviewer.

Authors believe that most book critics only read the 'blurb'—descriptive words inside the book jacket. This is not always true, though some reviewers give that impression. The essay book type review, a comparatively long article written by a reviewer, who knows something about the subject and can judge it from a standpoint of authority is a scholarly effort. Another type of review is feature article, is a piece put together from the contents of the book, but not offering a detailed judgment on it. This last is often written by a reporter who will treat the story told by the book as he would treat any other news story.

Freelancing

Freelancing is becoming common these days. In district towns particularly, a reporter works for several newspapers at the same time. He not only sends news, but also writes special features and articles for print media and also for radio. Besides, he may perhaps be working in an independent job on regular basis. Freelancers are paid according to the number of words per article.

At times freelance contributors are journalists—specialists who work for several newspapers on subjects for which regular staff reporters cannot be employed. Some people take to freelancing because it gives them an opportunity to pursue different plans, schedule their own time and work on their choice of subjects.

A freelance journalist or a photographer is not employed by one organisation. He is paid for each piece of assignment by the organisation for which he works. A freelancer is free to produce news stories for several publications, none of which is a full-time employer.

One of the well-known development journalists, Bharat Dogra, who contributes articles to several newspapers and magazines, says: "If someone asked me the main reason for selecting freelance journalism as a career, my immediate response would be to describe the opportunities this career provided for carrying out extensive and sustained research in areas of one's liking as its most important asset. If, for example, I am interested in protection of forests and related subjects, as a freelance journalist, I get the opportunity for studying this subject over a period of several years, meeting the officials and social workers involved in the protection of forests and visiting various forest areas."

However, the life of a freelance journalist is not easy. Freelance journalists have to pitch stories to various publications to get approval from the editor for their story ideas. Once the story idea is approved, the journalist has to research, meet and interview people and travel. He may have to take photographs also as part of his assignment. All this involves time, effort and money.

Newspaper Language

Throughout the book an attempt has been made to stress the quality of newspaper language. The first chapter discussed language for reporting—short words, short sentences, short paragraphs, avoiding long windedness, and to keep writing direct and specific. It has, however, been seen that sentences in the newspapers often become clumsy because the reporters want to cram too many points. A single sentence of a number of lines forms one paragraph. One paragraph involves a number of names. There are also instances of total lack of editorial co-ordination where the same photograph is printed on facing pages in the same edition of the same newspaper on the same day. Some of the examples are given to point out flaws. Efforts have been made not to mention the name of the reporter or the newspaper. Any identification would be merely incidental.

Where the name of the newspaper or the reporter does get identified, sincere apologies are offered. The reason for doing so is only to aid the students and teachers of journalism to avoid pitfalls.

Text Comments

1. While an official spokesperson has clarified that the Pakistan President, Pervez Musharraf, was not referring to the possible use of nuclear weapons, when he was said to have warned the Prime Minister,

Atal Bihari Vajpayee, that a resort to non-conventional methods of war should not be ruled out if Indian troops crossed the border, there remains sufficient ambiguity to suggest that Islamabad has not abandoned its practice of raising the nuclear bogey from time to time. (First Editorial, 3 January, 2003)

2. Having realized that the private sector was playing a creative role in the promotion of standard education, the state government, which was in the process of evolving a new education policy, was likely to involve private resources and introduce the contract system for teachers for strengthening the infrastructure and for making schools, colleges and universities really function in accordance with the changing world education scenario and the needs of the people. (2 December, 2002)

Editing

Text

3. Giving an indication that the new education policy might see private participation, Mr. Surinder Singla, Chairman of the High-powered Advisory Committee on Fiscal Reforms and Financial Reconstruction and Resource Mobilisation, constituted by the Punjab Government, told *The Tribune*, that having known that the private sector's performance was excellent in the field of education; Chief Minister Capt. Amarinder Singh was actively involved in evolving the new education policy with an objective to put Punjab ahead and achieve a higher economic growth rate. (Second para of the same news report)

4. What stunned 22 year-old Sony and her younger sister Jeeta (name changed) saw the changed behaviour of family acquaintances constables Kulwinder Singh and Davinder Singh, attached to a local judicial officer, when they barged into their houses in an inebriated state at about 4 p.m. when the two sisters were alone at their houses as their mother had gone to Delhi to receive her third daughter who was coming from England. (21 November, 2002; Front page news)

5. The election for this Assembly segment, to be held on April 4, seems to have become a fight between the Punjab Chief Minster, Capt. Amarinder Singh and the former Chief Minister, Mr. Parkash Singh Badal, as the later has announced that the victory of the Congress-CPI

alliance candidate, M.N. Nathu Ram, is a prestige issue for him and Mr. Badal while predicting victory of SAD candidate, Mrs. Mukhtiar Kaur, claimed that poll outcome would be the beginning of the collapse of the present regime. (18 March, 2002)

Long sentence, several persons and their statements being commented upon 15-line single sentence, complicated construction.

Eighteen line single sentence paragraph, lengthy designation, confused message.

Single paragraph of 14-lines; almost all persons involved in the incident clubbed in one paragraph, too many connecting words. One paragraph of 16-lines, totally confusing, several names in one sentence makes the news item complicated.

Incidentally, the same reporter reported news items at 2, 3 and 4. In most of the cases the sentences/paragraphs should have been divided into two or three sentences. Only a bit of rewriting would have made the text more readable, and less complicated to understand.

REFERENCES

Bruce, D. Itule and Douglas A. Anderson (1994): *News Writing and Reporting for Today's Media*, McGraw-Hill Inc., New York.

Gregory, A Barnes (1986): *Write for Success*, ISI Press, Philadelphia.

George, T.J.S. (1989): Editing: *A Handbook for Journalists*, Indian Institute of Mass Communication, New Delhi.

The Media Foundation (1996): *Beyond Those Headlines*, New Delhi.

William F. Irmscher (1981): *The Holt Guide to English*, Holt, Rinehart and Winston, New York.

Appendix-I: Examples of Redundant Expressions

Long and unnecessary	Short and precise form
At the hour of sunset	At sunset
A box with a round shape	A round box
The actual fact	Fact
6 pm in the evening	6 pm
Detailed research	Research
Sing together in chorus	In chorus
Consensus of opinion	Consensus
True facts	Facts
And two alternatives	Alternatives
At an early date	Soon
Caused injuries to	Injured
Filled to capacity	Full
In addition to	Besides
In spite of the fact that	Despite
In the course of	During
Is of the opinion	Believes
Made good their escape	Escaped
One of the reasons	One reason
On account of the fact	Because
Placed under arrest	Arrested
Rendered assistance	Helped
Succumbed to his injuries	Died
Sustained injuries	Was injured
Under active consideration	Being considered

10

Public Relations

Subsidiary Journalism

In every country there are a number of institutions which have departments for press and publicity work, i.e. for public relations (PR). This kind of PR work is done by private institutions, such as companies and associations, as well as by administration, governments and political parties. Most of the growth in this area of journalism is happening not only in business enterprises, but in societal sphere as well.

There are hundreds of definitions of PR in the literature of mass communication. PR work is defined as "deliberate and legitimate effort to create understanding and to build and cultivate trust in pubic opinion on the basis of systematic research." PR is perceived as conscious, planned and ongoing effort to build mutual understanding and trust.

PR practitioners themselves argue that PR is neither advertising nor propaganda. PR is seen as one of the information sources which also serves the interests of the recipients, as opposed to advertising and propaganda which is essentially designed to manipulate the recipients.

PR is generally agreed to have started in the USA in the late 19th and early 20th century. It set out initially to counter criticism by writers, journalists and social critics of entrepreneurs and the representatives of big business preferring to do their dealing away from public scrutiny.

Former journalists were hired to polish poor company images. A former newspaperman, Ivy Lee, co-founder in 1905 of the 'Parker and Lee' public relations agency, was one of the leaders in the field. 'The Declaration of Principles' he drew up contained fundamental notions of PR work. To Lee, the main task of PR work was thoroughly and quickly to inform the public. In brief, our plan is, frankly and openly, on behalf of the business concerns and public institutions, to supply to the press and public of the United States prompt and accurate information concerning subjects which is of value to the public to know about. Lee was not satisfied to be a mere mouthpiece of the enterprises he served but urged his clients to re-examine their business policies and to correct wrong attitudes in order to create favourable public opinion and a more positive response in the press. Since then the purpose of public relations has not changed.

PR as a Profession

In the 1920s, PR became a full-time profession. Social institutions such as churches, trade unions and foundations also recognized the need to inform the public of their aims and activities. The public relations approach changed from a more or less defensive role to an initiating and ongoing activity.

Public relations cover a variety of activities that include: public information, public affairs, investor relations, corporate communications, employee relations marketing or product publicity and consumer service or customer relations. Whatever the term, the basic activity consists of communicating information about an organisation or an individual in the best light.

Efforts to Reach General Public: Efforts to reach the general public by means of PR can be divided into two fields. Direct PR attempts to influence the public by special publications, e.g. customer journals, leaflets, personal contact, advertising etc.... Indirect PR uses the general mass media. To this end press releases are issued, press conferences held or events interesting and newsworthy to the media organized. Here the source of information does not remain passive but takes the initiative in addressing the media. In responding to public relations, the journalist is no longer active gatherer of information but has a mediating function in that he/she publishes, information material made available. In his book, *Concept of Journalism*, Michael Kunçzik says:

> *The mass media has become largely dependent on the information offered by these organizations and institutions.*

> *PR has evolved from a passive, originally defensive information source to an active information producer whose output is increasingly used by journalists, more and more of whom are doing without research of their own.*

Researches conducted by Swiss and German media organizations in the past have shown that between 73 per cent and 90 per cent of the material selected for publication was printed without comment. In most cases, any editing consisted merely of shortening and/or unimportant reformulations (e.g. conversion from direct to indirect speech, text re-sequencing etc.). There was practically no trace of journalistic self-initiative. In another case, it was found that the writers of press releases succeed in making work easier for the journalists. The releases were written in agency style—the most important facts up top, then descending order of importance so that they could be taken over without much editing and can be cut from the bottom up.

This happened with 71 per cent of the handouts offered, with the agency in most cases only cutting or reformulating, but largely keeping to the gist and language of the PR original. Once such a handout has gone past the news agency it is very likely to be published by the agency's clients which are newspapers, radio and television.

Handout Journalism: Since journalists rarely reveal the sources and the readers, listeners and viewers—cannot recognize the dependence of media on PR. Often the media are credited with what has actually resulted from PR work. PR can control not only the themes but also the timing of reporting because almost 70 per cent of the information is passed on immediately, i.e. on the next possible day, by news agencies, the press, radio and television. Contrary to how journalists like to see their role, PR shapes media output to an enormous extent.

It has been seen that in most of the cases the journalists accept information only too readily. Partisan information is accepted unquestioned and passed on as an allegedly genuine journalistic product. Such a situation may result in relying too much on handout journalism. Handout is a general term for a news story originating from public relations or public information sources. The term reflects the fact that the press releases or press notes are literally handed out to the media.

Handouts or press releases are a valuable source of news. However, they must be screened carefully for their news value. Many handouts are too biased, one-sided and partisan or too insignificant to be used. Journalists would do well to remember that it is for them to verify the information or data being claimed in the press handouts. They should not accept every information contained therein as a matter of routine. Official claims of 'achieving targets' need to be suitably verified.

It would be highly improper, and even unethical for journalists to go by whatever is dished out by the PR persons. It should be remembered that while the PR personnel are bound to stand by the official version, they may not be, for obvious reasons, telling the whole truth.

Sometimes, the PR persons have to defend the actions of their company or the administration which are palpably wrong. In that case journalists will have to go beyond the official version and investigate the truth. Relying on PR handouts would amount to being less than objective which is an important principle of journalism.

Relationship between PR and Media

The relationship between the media and public relations remains close. The press depends on public relations people for tips and information. As more people in public relations have journalism degrees and know news values, they can generally talk one-to-one with journalists.

Another evaluation of the public relations work says: The public relations worker and the journalist are interdependent. As much as a third to a half of all the material used by newspapers, broadcast stations, originates with a public relations or public information specialist. The journalist must rely on the accuracy and truth of the information supplied by the public relations specialist, especially since much of what is contained in press releases is accepted at face value.

In short, journalists rely on the pubic relations specialists to do their jobs honestly and fairly. This reliance is sometimes considerable because the public relations worker has access to sources that the reporter may not, and often the public relations person is a specialist in a field with which the reporter is only superficially acquainted. "Most of today's senior public relations practitioners started in journalism," says the Public Relations Society of America. "The experience gained in writing, personal contact, and other aspects of work for metropolitan or smaller newspapers, journals or trade magazines, and broadcasting media is still deemed important by a majority of public relations employers."

PR Consultants and Spin Doctors: Many political parties and corporate houses employ senior journalists as PR consultants for lobbying with the media so as to get favourable publicity and interpretation for their point of view.

A spin doctor is someone who is skilled in public relations and who advises political parties on how to engage in spin control by interpreting or reinterpreting situations that will reflect a more favourable or less damaging image. Journalists should be generally wary of such an effort which may be just a 'plant' in favour of their candidate or their party.

PR: A Link Between Public and Administration

Public relations is a means to eliminate misunderstanding and misgivings and promote healthy relationship between the public and administration. In a democratic set-up, public support is a prerequisite for an efficient administration. People should understand how they are being governed. Once they appreciate this, the government will find it easier to secure their support for participation in implementing its policies and programmes, thus ensuring quicker national development.

In a democratic society, the main factor responsible for development of public relations activities is the emergence of Parliament and the State Legislatures, elected on the basis of adult franchise. Increasing awareness of the people concerning government policies and programmes, discussions on government performance in open forum underscore the need for a strong public relations movement.

In India, professionalism in public relations started with the formation of professional organisations of public relations practitioners in various parts of the country. The Public Relations Society of India was formed in 1958 with a view to improving the standards of public relations in the country.

PR Set-up of the Central and State Governments

Soon after independence, the Ministry of Information and Broadcasting,

Government of India, was placed under the charge of a Minister of State for Information and Broadcasting. Special attention was paid to the public relations function under the democratic government of free India. The Central as well as State Governments carry out public relations function extensively. The Ministry of Information and Broadcasting of the Government of India is a massive organisation that feeds a lot of news and information to the media and hosts all press releases on its website.

Press Information Bureau: The Press Information Bureau (PIB), which is manned by the officers of the Indian Information Service, handles most of the press and publicity work of the ministries of the Central Government. The Principal Information Officers (PIOs) issue press releases, arrange interviews of the journalists with the senior officers and ministers, arrange press conferences and press parties.

The PIB is responsible for disseminating information about the policies and the programmes of the Central Government. PIB is the nodal agency of the Government to disseminate information to the print and electronic media on policies, initiatives and achievements. With five Zonal Offices, 19 Regional Offices and 16 Branch Offices, the PIB disseminates information through press releases, features, backgrounders and fact-sheets. It provides accreditation to journalists, arranges press conferences and organises media outreach programmes. It also provides photos, videos, e-booklets and infographics. The information material is released in English, Hindi and Urdu which is subsequently translated into other languages. PIB also arranges photo coverage of Government activities and the photographs are supplied to dailies and periodicals published in English and other Indian languages all over the country.

Likewise, at the State and the Union Territory levels, the Departments of Information and Public Relations, with varying nomenclatures, have established themselves as important means for publicizing government activities and developing awareness among the people regarding government plans and accomplishments. It in turn helps in obtaining people's reactions and opinions on such measures. The departments have sections which look after the print and electronic media, field publicity, publications and photographic cell. They maintain regular liaison with the media, hold press conferences, issue press notes on behalf of the state government and district administration.

Public Relations in Universities: Besides performing the traditional functions of teaching and research, an agricultural university has the mandate to serve the farming community at the grassroots level. An agricultural university serves a vast constituency—farmers including farmwomen, livestock keepers, administrators, agri-business organisations and policy makers. This vast constituency is naturally interested in keeping itself abreast of the latest information regarding new varieties released, new courses introduced, plant disease measures evolved, control of diseases in animals etc. This information need of the public can be met by an efficient extension agency and the public relations set-up.

A public relations office in most of the universities functions under the administrative control of the Vice-Chancellor or is attached to a senior officer in the university administration. It performs its allotted task through various means—maintaining liaison with the media by holding press conferences, issuing press notes and bringing out university newsletter. It also keeps the university authorities informed about the news published in various newspapers by supplying press clippings. Some of the other functions performed by a public relations set-up in a university include attending to the visitors from abroad/ outstations, arranging special coverage in the press of important events—university convocations, cultural programmes, conferences and miscellaneous work assigned by the Vice-Chancellor.

Organisational Handicaps: These public relations offices render valuable assistance both to the public and the administration. However, in several cases they suffer from serious organizational handicaps—lack of requisite facilities and access to policy-making levels where important decisions are taken. At times important news sources are reluctant to pass on sensitive news to the public relations staff and, instead, pass on directly to the newsmen, resulting in the public relations office being sidelined. In such cases its effectiveness is eroded.

A public relations office, as is the case with any other organisations, would be effective only to the extent to which it is equipped with proper facilities and has trained staff. It should also have access to the principal executive officer and policy making levels from where the news actually emanates. In several universities, faculty members working in the Departments of Journalism and Mass Communication are entrusted with the responsibility of PR work. It has been the experience of the author, who has also worked additionally as PRO and Adviser Public Relations, that a faculty member who has the essential writing skills, nose for news and requisite dedication can serve the institution in image building and as a link between the press and the administration.

Press Conference: A press conference, also called news conference, is a meeting held generally by ministers, well-known political leaders, heads of corporate bodies, and other important persons to give information and answer journalists' questions. Press conferences are also arranged when heads of important institutions or administrative heads of public enterprises take over and wish to meet the press to convey their thinking on important issues. Political parties often arrange press conferences to release manifestos, offer reactions on matters of public importance or make important announcements about party policies and programmes.

Another objective of calling a press conference may be that people in public life seek publicity and wish to gain maximum exposure to newspaper readers and also on television and radio. These days press conferences are becoming media events in themselves and are quite often televised. The daily press briefings by the Ministry of External Affairs during the Kargil conflict were live telecast. They were attended by senior correspondents from the national press, as also by representatives of the foreign media, including international wire services. The press conference, organized every year at the time of budget presentation, where the Minister and officials of Finance Ministry offer clarifications to the queries from pressmen, is considered an important media event.

A major difficulty in news-gathering at a press conference is that generally a reporter is not allowed to ask more than one or two questions. If a reporter wishes to develop an in-depth story he may not be able to do so.

A Reporter's Dos and Don'ts for PR and Press Conferences

1. With respect to public relations, a reporter should not take

the story as it is. He should gather more information, rewrite the story and present it in his own way and style.

2. A reporter should develop healthy skepticism towards information coming from PR companies. Many PR persons and politicians convey stories in such a way that reporters send the news across without realizing that it was a plant and originally come from them and not from the reporter.
3. A reporter should research the subject and background of the press conference thoroughly. In that case he will be able to frame relevant questions.
4. He should highlight major points in the statement and also in question and answer period. Quite often the lead comes not from the statement but from the response to a question.
5. A reporter should listen to the other questions and answers, just in case unexpected come up.

After you have attended a number of press conferences these guidelines would have become a part of your working order. Till then keep these in mind and see to what extent you can implement at least some of these.

REFERENCES

Bruce, D. Itule and Douglas A. Anderson (1994): *News Writing and Reporting for Today's Media*, McGraw-Hill Inc., New York.

Gupta, V.S. and Indu Grover (1996): *Study Material for the Participants in Refresher Course on Communication Skills and Reporting*, Haryana Agricultural University.

Melvin, Mencher (1999): *Basic News Writing*, Universal Book Stall, New Delhi.

Michael, Kunczik (1986): *Concept of Journalism*, Friedrich Ebert Stiftung, Bonn.

11

Radio and Television News

Adhering to the Tenets of Journalism

Broadcasting on Radio and Television is an effective means of mass communication and continues to be popular despite the presence of the numerous digital media. Even underdeveloped areas have a transistor radio which serves as a link with the rest of the world. With the advent of satellite broadcasting, it has become possible to knit the world and relay information from anywhere to everywhere on the globe.

The techniques of writing and production for Radio and Television are different. In the case of radio, sound is the only medium, while for television visuals are equally, if not more, important. Naturally, the entire set of practices and techniques for telecasting has to be viewed differently from the one for broadcasting. Pictures and sound in TV must synchronize in order to create a single, unified effect. For Radio, one has to depend exclusively on speech and sound.

Radio writing demands a high degree of professional skill and competence. There is no room for anything but the absolute essential facts. Sentences must be simple and short. The listener cannot re-read a sentence if he does not understand it. Once it has been broadcast, the sentence is lost for ever. Anything which makes it difficult for the listeners to understand is bad radio. The main advantage of radio news is its speed. A story can be broadcast even as it breaks out. Unlike the newspaper reader, a radio listener has no time to reflect. He cannot afford to ask: "What was it that he just said," because, even as he asks the question he loses the bit that is being read.

The BBC is praised for its insistence on objectivity and accuracy, 'so far as is humanely possible'. A veteran broadcaster said: "It is bad to miss a deadline but worse not to have checked the story properly." The BBC staff are trained from the beginning to set aside their personal beliefs and to try to achieve political and social neutrality. An example of how the fast BBC correspondents work is the way the news of the demolition of the Babri Masjid in Ayodhya was flashed within a few minutes of its happening while the domestic radio was still far behind with the news. At that stage the position was still confused and the picture was not clear, but the BBC was out with the news of the demolition, because that was the most important thing.

Qualities of a Radio Programme

Lionel Fielden, the first Controller of Broadcasting in India, in a talk on 'Broadcasting as a Career,' in 1938 said: Broadcasting deals with every subject under the sun, the man who makes a success of it must be, in the best sense of the word, a dilettante; he must take interest in, and know something, about everything... . The Programme staff of a broadcasting station is in the same position as the editor of a newspaper who can make an exciting column out of a dull item of news, or a film producer who can twist a boring story into a first rate picture... the first necessity of those who wish to join the programme staff of broadcasting is precisely this infinite quality of being able to make bricks without straw, or if you like to put in another way, a special type of creative imagination. A radio programme should, therefore, have elements of intellectual curiosity and imaginative ability.

Writing for Radio

1. Use simple words without resorting to difficult language. Ensure that the sentences are not cluttered with unnecessary words.
2. Keep sentences short so that a listener can grasp what you are saying. Prefer active voice while writing.
3. Minimize the use of abbreviations in a radio script. Do not use symbols in the script. For example, instead of '10%', write '10 per cent'.

4. Add familiarity and humour in the script. Keep the script conversational so that a listener is not bored.
5. Keep just one idea per sentence. Avoid commas and conjunctions so as not to confuse the audience.
6. Do not try to influence your personal likes, dislikes, benefits, attributes etc.
8. Mention time required on the script.

Recording Radio Programmes

1. Keep your script ready.
2. Do not staple the papers but keep them arranged. So that when the recording of each page is over, papers of the script can be kept aside without noise.
3. Start when the signal of the recording is given by the technician.
4. Keep your voice at the room level.
5. Maintain normal speed of the speech.
6. The delivery of speech should be fluent and unhesitating.
7. Be at ease before the mike.
8. If you have cough or irritation in the throat, signal the operator so that he puts off the mike.
9. Modulate your voice well to make your broadcast effective and interesting.
10. Avoid any kind of noises, such as of turning papers or bangles etc.

Writing News for Radio

Writing news for radio is different from writing it for the newspaper. For radio, it has to be short, simple and direct, with familiar words and simple sentences. The news script has to be 'listenable' as the written word has to be 'readable'. Writing of news for radio has to be based on sound rather than sight. It follows the rules of good conversation. As far as the listener is concerned, radio news is spoken not read.

Because the medium is voice-to-ear, the general principle for writing for radio is: 'Write it as you would say it to a group of people.'

In his book, *Writing for Farm Families*, M.G. Kamath, illustrates the difference between the two types of news writing with the following example.

Readable: The Uttar Pradesh Government today proposed the establishment of four new fertilizer plants with a capacity of 1.8 million tons a year to meet the state's requirements of fertilizers in the Fourth Plan period.

Listenable: The Uttar Pradesh Government today proposed to set-up four fertilizer factories. The four factories together will produce 1.8 million tons of fertilizers a year. This quantity of fertilizers is needed by the state in the Fourth Plan period.

Writing for radio involves rewriting the script, sometimes many times over because news bulletins need to be constantly updated. Rewriting is essential to avoid monotonous repetition. It is also important to include audio actualities. Actualities are of two types.

Actualities

1. Audio actuality, which is pre-recorded sound, is used in a newscast. For instance, a radio reporter may record an interview with a consumer activist about the implementation of the Consumer Protection Act. He may then select a short 20 second portion of the interview for use in the news bulletin.
2. Live actuality is used when the actual voice of the consumer activist (in this particular case as above) is heard 'live' in the news bulletin.

While print journalism has the Five Ws (namely—Who, What, When, Where and Why), broadcast journalism has Four Cs (namely—Correctness, Clarity, Conciseness and Colour).

These four Cs serve as the basis for broadcast writing and form a good framework for our discussion here. One important characteristic of writing for broadcast is the emphasis on the immediate. Broadcast news must be up to the minute. While the past tense for verbs is preferred in the print media the present tense is preferred when news is broadcast concurrently with the event happening.

Consequently, newspaper story has to use past tense as the print begins after the event. For example, in a newspaper we will have an item "The Prime Minister said yesterday that he would support the hiking of petrol prices...."

The broadcast news story if related when the PM is making the speech in the Parliament will use present tense, e.g. "The Prime Minister says he supports a hike in petrol prices."

Broadcast news should be written for the ear, not the eye. The writer should bear in mind that someone is going to read the news and others are going to listen to him/her.

Broadcast news stories must gain the attention of the listeners from the beginning. The first words in the story are extremely important. Getting the attention of the listener is sometimes more important than summarizing the story or giving the most important facts of the story.

Interviewing for Radio

Generally, there are three types of interviews: spot interviews, field interviews and studio interviews. Spot interviews are brief and usually limited in scope.

"Who will you vote for?"

"As a passenger, how do you rate the service?"

Field interviews can be either long or brief. You may interview a farmer in his farm; a pilot at the airport.

Studio interviews are usually formal. Again, this may either be long or short.

Emotional interviews need sensitive handling. An interviewer must consciously stop him/herself from exploiting vulnerable situations and intruding into private grief.

Stories written for radio and television are written in conversational style, clearly and simply so that the listener or viewer can easily understand the story. Complicated news stories are simplified by emphasizing only one or two themes. Leads are short and the present tense is used whenever possible. Attribution is usually placed first in the sentence so that the listener or the viewer knows at once the source of information.

The first rule of broadcast news is that the story must be clear at once. Unlike the reader, the listeners have no second chance to go over the material. "Radio and Television news is written on the wind—here for the instant, then gone," says Melvin Mencher in his book, *Basic News Writing*.

Broadcast news writers use everyday words, the language of conversation. Colloquialisms are acceptable. The style is informal. The story written to be read plunges right into the heart of the event. Most of the sentences are short, much shorter than the sentences would be in the same story written for a newspaper. He says: Broadcast news has been described as a headline service. It is intended to give the listener or viewer only an outline of the event. A half-an hour news bulletin will not fill in the front page of a newspaper.

Broadcast writers frequently use the present tense in their leads. Newspapers stories almost always contain the past tense throughout. The reason for using the present tense is simple. Broadcast news is supposed to give the listeners or viewers the sense of immediacy or events being covered as they happen.

Radio Discussion

Radio discussion usually involves several participants and the moderator. The discussions are usually over issues and events that are of importance to the common man.

Radio discussions could be on any subject: politics, medicine, science, sports, literature. Some of the subjects could be:

(i) Shifting paradigm in development planning;
(ii) Public apathy to senior citizens; and
(iii) Introducing new fertilizers.

The moderator should carefully structure the discussion. The participants for the discussion programme should be experts in their field and selected with great care, the moderator should be non-partisan and ensure that everyone has an equal chance.

Rise of the News Channels

Television became a dominant force in India in the 1990s and with the launch of private television channels, it filled a major news gap for non-literate masses. Another reason why television became a major hit with people was its capacity to provide a wholesome package of news, information, current affairs, debates, serials, reality shows, entertainment and music. All of this got amplified once foreign television channels arrived on the Indian scene. Because television is different than the print medium and also radio, working for television calls for a slightly different set of skills for the journalist.

As television is a multi-media medium, people find it attractive and automatically easy to comprehend. But this very quality turns it into a difficult process that necessitates the involvement of an experienced team which can shoot, edit the videos, write a script and turn the entire venture into a full package. With 24-hour news channels, journalists and editors are always on their toes. Considering that videos are the mainstay of television news, the focus remains on getting good visuals and often the quality of visuals may decide the importance of a news item. Script writing for television requires a different kind of effort as the scripts are written and re-written with care so as not to repeat in audio what the visuals show but bolster the visuals by adding additional information.

Before scripting for TV programmes, it is essential to research the subject, visit various locations and sites and have a feel of the general environment and atmosphere. This exploration of all aspects, including requirement of the crew and duration of their stay, logistics, costs etc., need to be adequately undertaken. This exercise is called recce. The primary objectives of recce are to enable the writer to develop the outline sufficiently so as to have a proper idea of programme production.

Scripting for Television

Use simple language: Those who write news broadcasts must be good at the use of language so that the script is comprehensible to the audience. The language must be simple and direct with minimum use of complicated words or vocabulary so that the masses can understand easily.

Blending visuals and scripts: The essential part of a TV script is that the visual component is very important. Equally essential is the careful blending of both—the audio and video components—so as to bring harmony to the complete package.

Conversational language: The language of television is friendly, conversational and informal. It is not flamboyant and ostentatious like an article in a newspaper or a magazine. This is important also because the news reader should be at ease in reading out a script and not have to struggle with words.

Delete superfluous words: Any extra and unimportant information is eliminated at the first instance in a television story. This helps in keeping the emphasis on the main points in a news story.

Writing style: The writing style should be easy, direct and without any flourish and complexity.

REFERENCES

Indira Gandhi National Open University (1991): *Writing for Radio—Reaching the Public*, New Delhi.

Melvin Mencher (1999): *Basic News Writing*, Universal Book Stall, New Delhi.

Parthasarathy, Rangaswami (1994): *Here is the News: Reporting for the Media*, Sterling Publisher Pvt. Ltd., New Delhi.

12

Media in the Digital Age

News in Your Pocket

Information and Communication Technologies (ICTs) have impacted almost every walk of life. The transformation has been profound and unprecedented. The advent of information technology has dramatically changed almost all aspects of mass media—right from news gathering to editing, production to printing, and editing to broadcasting. This has happened not just for the print media but also for radio and television. Technology has also revolutionized not only the methods of news gathering but also the way newspapers are produced. Not since Gutenberg's invention of movable types in the 15th century has there been an innovation, so sweeping in nature, which has revolutionised communication as has computerisation.

This change wrought by ICTs is reflected at home and office, in personal and social communication, in the consumption of media and the production of media by the common people. The impact has also been felt because there are so many new ways of consumption, production and dissemination of news and information that have come into play, courtesy the internet, mobile phones and the supporting applications. The democratising forces that ICTs have unleashed in the world of media have effectively seen journalism slipping from the hands of a few to many. While the masses may have found a voice, it does not necessarily mean that the social media space has become wiser or clearer or more truthful. With the proliferation of technologies, the social media space just might have become cloudy and confusing.

With the younger generation growing up with gadgets and technology on its finger tips, the transformation in the mediascape has been phenomenal. Just ten years back, breaking news was a new phenomenon as television anchors and news-readers shouted out the latest happenings on the news front. The same channels, which had given stiff competition to newspapers, are competing with websites, social media platforms and the mobile phone to announce 'breaking news' first. Just recall how many times news about a riot or an earthquake is first announced on social media platforms like Twitter, Facebook or even Instagram than a news website or a TV channel. Breaking news is no longer rare bacause important events are being telecast simultaneously by many news organisations and even people. The pace of producing news and information and sharing it has become ultra easy and convenient. Anyone with a mobile phone can actually spread or share a piece of information globally within a few hours.

This process of technological change has been long and developed in stages. Let us look at the technological and other changes that impacted journalism and the print media. Desktop publishing has been called the grandchild of the typewriter and the child of the electronic typewriter. The advent of desktop publishing in the nineties resulted in the deployment of screen-based 'WYSIWYG' (What You See Is What You Get), a comprehensive design, layout and production package that effectively resulted in the cut and paste methodology being completely outdated.

Desktop publishing effectively allowed a single person to be able to run a publishing company from his desk. It enabled a single person to do everything that was normally done by many people in a publisher's office—writing the material, choosing the font type, designing the pages and producing the finished pages on a printer. Desktop publishing was enormously advanced for a busy office, looking at ways to produce much of its day-to-day printing needs quickly and cheaply.

The main advantage of desktop publishing was that it enabled well laid out documents from balance sheets to bus timetables to be laid out without a long learning process for the operator. Whatever is being planned, it can be set up on the computer screen and rearranged as many times as you like until it is perfect. Only then it is sent to the printer—and the printer in most cases is a machine on the table next to the computer.

Desktop publishing should be seen as a continuing process which began when the first typewriter was invented more than 140 years ago and then progressed and improved until the electronic typewriter came in some 40 years ago. As the computer age dawned and helped do everything from sending men to the moon to greatly improve medical skills, it was only natural that computers would find their way into offices and so was desktop publishing born. The actual date of the world's first desktop system being used was January 28, 1985 by Paul Brainerd, president of a company called the Aldus Corporation at its annual stockholder's meeting. Aldus became one of the big names in the DTP business.

As DTP gained acceptability, it brought about a revolution in the printing industry. More and more establishments which were not related to the media industry began using this versatile software-hardware combination that made designing simple and convenient. The result was that organisations began producing newsletters, magazines, posters and stationery all by themselves which gave them a more credible and professional personality. Even educational institutions like technical colleges, polytechnics, universities and other institutions began using DTP for a number of purposes like the production of college magazines, design of course materials and incorporating graphics such as maps, pictures and diagrams with ease.

Internet Journalism

Fast on the heels of desktop publishing came the internet revolution which has changed not just the media industry but also impacted society, politics and communication both at the local level as well as the global level. The internet is a global electronic community of millions of interconnected computer networks joined together through telephones, mobile phones and satellites. It means that millions of people are linked together on what has been aptly termed as the "information superhighway". What is remarkable about the internet is that it is loosely governed with little controlling authority for it. Yet, starting from a small network set by the US Defence Department, the internet has grown into a truly international supermarket.

The internet has done to the entire media industry what cable television had done to the print media—made the pace of news faster, sleeker and swifter. This is what the internet did to all of the media industry—introduce 24-hour news updates and bring the entire world on to a single global platform. After the advent of the internet, people did not have to wait for news till the next news bulletin or the newspaper the next morning. Moreover, when news websites came up and e-zines began to provide both news and features, it was all free. People stopped newspaper subscriptions as they took to reading news on websites—sitting at their office desks or at home on personal computers.

On the other hand, the mainstream media had to feed their websites with news constantly. Their once-a-day cycle of publishing news transformed to providing news constantly and updating news 24-hours. Steadily, millions of people began to switch over to the newer, faster and interactive sources of news. For instance, over 1.1 million users accessed the MSNBC website on August 17, 1998 for the top story on the Clinton-Lewinsky Affair, when the US President addressed the nation on his relationship with Lewinsky. This record was broken when more than two million people accessed the site on September 12, 1998 when the Star Report was made public. On the same day, CNN interactive reported three lakh hits a minute on its website even before the report was on the net.

Some of the websites are going beyond their print counterparts. Newspapers follow a 24-hour cycle, so do their internet editions. But since internet is such a live medium, news sites are experimenting to keep pace with news in some ways. The online publications are a sort of value-added product. The online medium also gave the media a number of opportunities to extend their reach to their audience and provide services like 'news by e-mail', where readers indicate the subjects of their interest and the website emails them the daily news bulletin or a weekly bulletin.

A typical newsroom has already undergone a lot of change due to the internet. Noisy teleprinters have been replaced with PC-based tickers. Television sets have become an integral part of the news room set-up.

Reporting and news gathering too were impacted because of the changing nature of news. It was no more life as usual for newspaper reporters. Earlier, a reporter would be out in the field during the day, meeting sources, conducting interviews and visiting a news spot, coming back only by evening to file the story. But with the coming of websites, the nature of reporting began to change—with reporters relaying updates and developments from the spot so that the organisation could update the website instantly. However, the reporter would still come back to file their stories for the next morning's newspaper.

As developing websites became easy, coders, designers and technologists came up with various kinds of Content Management Systems (CMS), that allowed easy control and updation of websites. The CMS proved to be a boon for many organisations as it allowed almost anyone to start a website. Small companies, NGOs as well as professionals made their own websites so that they could keep the world informed about their activities. The website became a global platform for people to showcase their skills and sell their services to the world.

Another Internet Revolution: The internet forced all kinds of media companies—newspapers, magazines, news agencies, radio and television channels—besides publishing houses and advertising firms to set up their websites. In just about a decade this trend and technology evolved to make way for better websites which were more dynamic and interactive. These websites eventually led to social media websites. Called Web 2.0, this fast-paced change put unparalleled power in the hands of the reader as technology, gadgets and ideas came together to unfold a revolution in the media industry.

The most formidable challenge to the traditional media has been put up by technology companies and non-traditional news companies. With more and more news websites catering to different kinds of readers and audiences, the news scenario has undergone a tremendous change. Even the Press Council of India (PCI) foresaw the impact of multiple technology systems as a result of convergence of technologies. It quotes V. Parikh, Executive Director, Centre for News Media as saying: The digital technology and advances in the telecommunication facilities would aid journalistic advancement. No longer could a journalist remain "isolated" and content to remain in a one-dimension medium.

It is no wonder that newspapers and magazines of the 21st century are now present everywhere—on the web as well as on the various social media platforms. That online journalism is making headway in disseminating information to the masses is clear from the way it has been playing a major role in last few general elections in India. After the news and organisational websites, it were the social media websites like Facebook and Twitter, along with search engines that changed the face of journalism and media. With more and more young people logging in and setting up accounts on social media, news organisations realised that a lot of readers had shifted to these platforms. It was natural that newspapers, magazines, TV channels and radio stations followed the people to the social media. This space became more interactive with readers giving feedback straight to the journalists. Not just this, they held debates with the mainstream media and engaged with them in a way that had not been imagined earlier.

The internet domain remained dynamic with a number of players coming in and shutting shop. Many ruled the news scene for some time and then whittled down. In the early years, we had players like www.rediff.com, www.yahoo.com that ruled the roost but they gradually lost ground to the newer and smarter players. Yahoo and Rediff became aggregators of news and drew stories from online editions of other newspapers and even news agencies like PTI and IANS besides foreign media like BBC and CNN. They separated news from opinion columns and editorials to provide a wholesome dose of daily information to their readers.

Now, established journalists and media companies prefer to launch news websites instead of starting newspapers or magazines. In fact, many owners have decided to close down newspapers and concentrate on running news websites only. Many websites try to carve out a niche by not focusing on routine news but only on exclusives and opinion articles. Some of the new websites that have made a mark in Indian journalism include https://theprint.in, https://thewire.in, https://www.thequint.com and https://www.firstpost.com.

Even Abdul Kalam, the great scientist and President of India, launched his own website to share his thinking and views about India's future—www.abdulkalam.com. Similarly, all government agencies, departments and ministries have opened a direct interface with the citizens through not just websites but through other digital interfaces like apps and emails.

The next big change after websites and social media has been the squeezing of the internet into the smart phone, literally making magic with this revolutionary idea. This small device has metamorphosed into a voice recorder, camera, phone and laptop, allowing people to produce information and content from the spot. The mobile has given a voice even to people who are not literate. Now, they can click images through their cameras, make changes to these through various apps and share these with their network and on their social media in a jiffy. By recording their voice, they can share their opinion easily, everywhere. The phone, powered with the internet and a variety of apps has become a powerful tool in the hands of the public for the production and dissemination of that information.

The Rise and Rise of Fake News

The democratising effect of the convergence of technology and gadgets that gave people a voice and led to an interactive process also created a Frankenstein in the form of fake news. With people getting the power to create and share information instantly, many also resorted to making mischief. What aided the spread of fake news was the mobile—the hand held device which allowed people to produce and share fake and misleading news instantaeously. The scourge of fake news was seen particularly during and around election time. WhatsApp was detected as a major culprit that led to people sharing information instantly to groups of people. A phenomenon that shook not just India but enveloped the entire world, often sending people into a tizzy as news of the deaths of many eminent people was reported often. By the time the masses would realise that the information about the death of a popular celebrity is fake, it would have travelled across continents, reaching tens of millions and eroding the credibility of the mainstream media and journalists.

In early 2018, Facebook CEO Mark Zuckerberg, who had bought WhatsApp, said that India had over 200 million users of WhatsApp. A large of these users were propagators and the victims of fake news peddled over WhatsApp. So, why is it that the nuisance of fake news is no longer a nuisance but a serious problem for the country. Because, fake and wrong news with ulterior motives has led to riots and violence, creating serious tension in society. It has also led to severe erosion of the credibility of the media along with seeding mistrust amongst the masses about everything that is political, religious and social—posing a threat to democracies. One weapon that has been deployed repeatedly by the creators of fake news has been the use of old and unrelated photographs and videos with false information and exaggerated claims.

Some examples of fake news:

- A photograph of cattle dying in Rajasthan. This image was taken from Kenya but put in an Indian context to create tension in the public.
- That the new Rs. 2,000 note has a micro-chip implanted in it so that investigative agencies can track the hoarding of black money.
- That Sonia Gandhi, the leader of the Congress party is richer than Queen Elizabeth of the UK.
- That prosthetic fingers are being used by people to be able to vote many times.
- A photograph of Jawaharlal Nehru being kissed by his niece was passed off as a foreign woman kissing Nehru.
- A four-decade old photograph of Kiran Bedi being invited for tea by a generous Prime Minister Indira Gandhi immediately after her car was towed to compare her with Narendra Modi and portray him as being a vengeful Prime Minister.

Writing for the Web

More and more journalists are writing for the web—for news websites, personal blogs and even the social media platforms. They are not just writing but are actually creating a diverse range of content. The digital medium requires not just articles, but also photographs, infographics, hyperlinks and interactive designing so that a reader can easily understand and navigate a website.

On the other hand, web users tend to scan news pages, instead of spending time reading news to find out what interests them. Writing for the web needs a different style because people use websites and social media differently as compared to the traditional media. Therefore, for a web journalist it is important to ensure that his opening words—the intro, is sharp and interesting. Some of the basic rules for web writing are:

- Write in brief. Use simple and direct language because the Internet users want quick and short information.
- Write correct facts and figures. Always check and re-check from credible sources of information.
- Be specific in your writing.
- Remember that grammar is important even on social media and websites. Therefore, do not overuse exclamation marks to emphasise your point. It is not like a radio or television where the listeners/viewers don't see your mistakes.
- Write is present tense. Do not use past tense nor future tense. This makes a story look new and immediate.
- News media writing uses active voice. Avoid use of passive voice.
- A reliable length for a story is 300-400 words. Most online readers do not want to read long articles.
- One paragraph on the web should be a minimum of two sentences and maximum of 4-5 sentences. Shorter posts lead to better engagement of users.
- Use visuals and also spacing. Provide a space between two paragraphs to give a visual break. Separately, provide relevant images to hold the interest of the user in your story.
- Use maps, graphs and infographics to illustrate your stories. You can make complicated figures easier to understand by making a graph or a chart.
- An important part of working on the web is to learn new software, online tools and apps.
- Provide links to medias.

The march of information technology, coupled with the rise of the internet and powered by the ever-evolving mobile phone is relentless. The benefits of information technology and print media modernization are very much visible. The proliferation of language newspapers, the colour explosion and the specialized journals are the results of new technology. Even publishing and printing have become much easier. Now a whole manuscript can be written on a computer and sent through an e-mail. No hassle of going through the tedious time consuming and lengthy process of composing, proof reading and page-making time and again.

REFERENCES

British Council (2001): *A Manual of Human Rights Reporting in India*, Press and People, New Delhi.

Press Council of India (2001): *Future of Print Media*, New Delhi.

Press Institute of India: *Vidura* (Various Issues): New Delhi.

The Media Foundation (1996): *Beyond Those Headlines*, New Delhi.

13

Communication Skills for Technical and Research Writing

Another Aspect of Media

The information technology revolution has resulted in a huge increase in the amount of information to be widely disseminated to end users. Research organisations, universities, corporate bodies and academic institutions require services of people who are capable of processing information and designing publications. Technical publications provide an interface between institutions, publishers and the end-users.

Technical writing introduces people to some of the most important aspects of writing in the world of science, technology and business. It deals with factual information, uses simple instead of emotional language, and caters to the intellect. Technical writing is, therefore, delivery of technical information to readers in a manner that is suited to their needs, level of understanding and background.

> "Technical style is characterized by a colon, restrained tone, an absence of any attempt to arouse emotion, use of specialized terminology, the use of abbreviations and symbols, and the integrated use of illustrations, tables, charts and diagrams to help exposition. Technical writing is characterized by exactness rather than grace or variety of expression. Its main purpose is to be informative and functional rather than entertaining. Thus, the most important qualities of technical writing are clarity, precision, conciseness and objectivity."
>
> (Weisman, H.M., *Basic Technical Writing,* Ohio: Charles E. Merrik Books, Inc. 1962.)

In an industrial society, where producers have to maintain continuing association with the buyers, technical writing has come into its own. Because of the increasing responsibility of technical writers in communicating information in simple, usable language these writers are being referred to as technical communicators.

The Communication Director for the Society for Technical Communication, Maurice Martin, explains, "Technical means having a good grasp of the complexity of the product, service or industry that you are covering and communications for both, explaining the issue and being able to work within a team."

The ability to convey technical information to a non-specialist is the key skill of a technical communicator. Most technical communicators in the Indian industry have come with a background in English language or journalism. The companies are, therefore, increasingly using the services of writers with good communication skills, knowledge of designing and capable of working as a team. The technical writer is a part of a team that designs, creates and markets a product. Such a person, therefore, must be able to work well with other people with varied backgrounds, and be able to communicate effectively with them.

The ability to design a document is an important responsibility in which a technical writer should be proficient. Document designing comprises a number of related activities ranging from checking the language for clarity and comprehension, formatting the text, and ensuring uniformity in style and presentation. A technical communicator should also be able to design various kinds of publications—folders, brochures, newsletters, annual reports and other publishing material.

Language for Technical and Research Publications

Each profession has its own jargon, so does science and technology. As different disciplines of science and technology develop, each creates its own vocabulary which is understood only by those routinely using it. The aim of the language used should be lucidity and not profundity. Science writing in newspapers and periodicals is entirely different from articles published in specialized journals. The technical and science writers need to make the subject comprehensible even to a layman. One difficulty that the scientists and academicians face is that they take the desire of the audience to learn for granted and forget to do their part of the bargain: to make the subject interesting and as easy to understand as possible. Scientists themselves are not always conscious of the fact that their professional terminology may not be clear to the common people. Their main concern is their work and not communication. One of the reasons why scientific journals and periodicals have very limited circulation is that the language used by them is too technical and, therefore, beyond the grasp of the average reader.

The simple rule of thumb is that just as you are not able to comprehend much of what is written by a specialist of another profession, a person who is not trained in your branch of specialization may be lost if you write in the standard language of your subject. For instance, an agricultural scientist may be able to communicate freely with another agricultural scientist, but he cannot make himself clear to a space scientist and *vice versa*. If this is the block that develops even among highly educated persons, things are all the more difficult when the matter has to be explained to a person who has no or little grounding in the particular subject. Therefore, a technical writer has to go out of his way to explain every phenomenon in the layman's language.

The shorter an article, the greater the chances that it will be read in full. So along with simplifying the language, one has to learn the art of condensing one's thoughts in minimum possible words. This requires considerable skills. Regular practice, attention to detail and patience are essential for developing basic skills in writing, document designing and copy editing—hallmarks of a successful technical communicator.

In this chapter our objective is to discuss important aspects of technical and research writing and manuscript preparation. Some of the important terms concerning research methods and methodology are given below:

Database: A database is basically a computerized record keeping system whose purpose is to store information and allow users to retrieve and update that information on demand. The information in question can be anything that is of significance to the individual or organisation concerned—anything, in other words, that is needed to assist in the general process of running the business of that individual or organisation.

Databases and database systems have become an essential component of everyday life in modern society. In the course of a day, most of us encounter several activities that involves interaction with a database. In the past few years, advances in technology have been leading to exciting new applications of database systems. Multimedia databases store pictures, video clips and audio files. Geographic information systems (GIS) can store and analyse maps, weather data and satellite images.

The advantages of a database system over traditional, paper-based methods of record keeping are as under:

- *Compactness:* There is no need for voluminous paper files.
- *Speed:* The machine can retrieve and update data far faster than a human can.
- *Less drudgery:* Much of the sheer tedium of maintaining files by hand is eliminated. Mechanical tasks are always better done by machines.
- *Currency:* Accurate, up-to-date information is available on demand at any time.

In journalism, databases serve a useful purpose because newspapers build libraries by putting their contents into a computer, as do magazines and research publications. Over the last decade, the government is also computerizing documents, along with court opinions and census reports. Database is specially useful because it saves time for reporters, provides the most recent information and allows access to information usually not available anywhere else. University libraries have databases on thesis, topics and dissertations while a medical institution may have a database on medicine.

Questionnaire: A popular method of data collection, a questionnaire basically consists of a series of questions designed to obtain factual information about people's attitudes, values, opinions, or beliefs about a particular subject or issue. A questionnaire can also be constructed so as to contain questions about a range of topics or issues. They are regularly used as a tool of market research and are central to understanding the audience. Questionnaires may be conducted in a variety of ways: for example, a researcher reading out the questions face-to-face to the respondent and filling in the responses.

Alternatively, a written questionnaire may be sent out and returned by post. Questionnaires are useful for gathering large amounts of data for investigating an issue in depth. But for smaller research and in rural areas the participants observation or interviews may be more useful.

Case study: It is generally a process in problem solving in which students, trainee supervisors, managers etc. examine a specific case with a view to arriving at a solution, either by action or by decision. An industrial case study might analyse a particular conflict, a breakdown in communication, offer an explanation of the dispute, and a way of solving it.

Forms of Publications

Staff members working in research institutes, universities and academic organisations are expected to produce publishable material as part of their job assignment. As a scientist, academic, or research worker, it is a part of one's duty to communicate the results of research to as wide an audience as possible. The work that is done in an institution becomes useless unless its results are disseminated widely to the public. Reliable research data buried in the files or gathering dust in the investigators' office does not serve public purpose. A research worker has the moral obligation to release promptly significant results of his research efforts.

Statement by Dr. Robert E. Yoder, Agricultural Research Administration Adviser, OSU-USAID Mission to Punjab Agricultural University, in a speech, titled, 'Publication and Dissemination of Research Results', delivered at the Second Agricultural University Workshop, February 18, 1965.

Publishing research increases knowledge, stimulates debate and encourages further work on the subject by opening up new opportunities for research. Many research articles that are published are of a high standard because these are peer reviewed before these are accepted for publication. Because of the high standards usually required of research articles, it is often difficult to have a paper accepted by a journal. Much research is done, but only a small amount is finally published (Fig. 13.1).

Of the total amount of research that is planned and started, only a small proportion is ever published, and for a number of reasons, an even smaller percentage is actually read by the people who can benefit most from the work.

Excerpted from: *Writing Research Papers—An Easy Guide for Non-Native English Speakers.*

Research Bulletins: Publications in research bulletins are relatively technical, detailed, scientific, and professional. They represent the highest level of scientific writing. Research bulletins contain new data, and new analyses or new conclusions. They establish the conclusions beyond doubt or questions. They should follow approved and adequate methods of analyses, should be prepared in clear, letter-perfect language. Such reports are generally much longer than is suitable for journal articles, and contain data and other material, which are complex and technical.

The responsibility for accuracy rests with the author. He must be extremely careful to check all data, making certain that all figures, mathematical calculations, and statistical representations have been reproduced without error. He is also responsible for the accuracy of his interpretations and conclusions, and for the clarity of expression in his manuscript to assure understanding by the audience. These are key stepping-stones to a professional reputation for reliability.

Distribution of research bulletins is generally limited to other researchers or professional people who are familiar with the vocabulary of research and technical communication.

Special Publications: All institutes occasionally need to publish reports and other materials that do not fit into research series or any of the other classifications. A good example of this special type of report would be a compilation of information of particular significance to a group of individuals who may be influential supporters of the institution.

Such reports are special-purpose publications, intended primarily for audience with specified needs or interests. These reports are most often semi-technical in form, are directed to an audience whose needs cannot be served adequately either by a technical or a simplified publication. Other examples of such audiences might be community level extension workers, vocational, agriculture or home science teachers, or special interest groups in business or industry.

Materials issued in public relations and promotional brochures might also be described as special reports. Some institutions have a policy of publishing interim, or progress reports on research, which is incomplete, or on a completed phase of a larger study. Other institutions use the term 'miscellaneous publications' to classify such materials.

Research Journal Papers: A research paper may be defined as a documented prose incorporating the results of an organized analysis of a subject. In its style, structure and approach, it closely resembles a formal report.

Research workers frequently have occasions to report some results of their studies to their fellow scientists and other interested persons. One good way to do this without writing a complete research report or bulletin, is to prepare an article for publication in a professional, scientific, or technical journal. Some journals could be the Indian Journal of Agricultural Science, the Indian Journal of Horticulture and also Communicator, which is brought out by the Indian Institute of Mass Communication. Articles for journals are based on research based, well suited to reporting and recording results, and scientific applications of research. Manuscript length and content depends upon the policy of the journal for which the article is written.

The author should make an effort for data presentation through tables, graphs, charts, photographs and info-graphics that require skilled execution. This is the author's responsibility, although he may not actually do the work of preparing the finished graphics. It is likely that the illustrations will be better if he hires a professionally trained designer for illustrations and data. However, the author should consult with and advise the artist and photographer so that the illustrations do the job intended.

Handbook: The *Collins Cobuild English Dictionary* defines a handbook as a book that gives you advice and instruction about a particular subject, tool or machine. Another definition is—a collection of useful information, combining some of the features of both a dictionary and an encyclopaedia. Professional organisations produce handbooks for different types of clientele—office staff, technical personnel, shareholders. A handbook should be convenient to handle.

The contents of a handbook are determined by its purpose and readership. Senior teachers, scientists and experts also bring out handbooks for students on different subjects. A good handbook should be a storehouse of information.

Manual: A manual is a guidebook or a workbook. It deals with a particular process or a procedure. An instruction manual with your computer or mobile phone or any other household gadget is essentially meant to help you understand the working of the machine. User manuals for consumer products are generally written in simple language so that they may make sense for whom these are meant.

A *Manual for Writers of Term Papers, Theses and Dissertations*, written by K.L. Turabian, is a valuable publication usually recommended to graduate students. *A Manual of Style*, published by the University of Chicago Press, is widely followed as a standard book for general writing. Likewise, laboratory manuals lay down procedure about performing specified experiments and give information regarding equipment, components and apparatus used in the laboratory.

So, the question is who produce these manuals? The answer is—the technical writers who research and write for such manuals in collaboration with designers and other team members. Therefore, it is important that a technical writer must acquaint himself with different kinds of manuals brought out by various organisations, including industrial houses. There is a wide scope of using one's ingenuity in designing, formatting and illustrating manuals so as to make these user-friendly.

Brochure: Used for marketing and promotions, a brochure gives a broad overview of an institution, organization or a department. It provides detailed information so as to satisfy the needs of a customer or a client. It serves the purpose of responding to general request for information on a department or an institution.

While starting work on a brochure, it is essential to discuss the theme of the brochure with persons associated with the organization and note down ideas and developments from the head of the organization and the team. Then organize ideas and write them down in an informative form. Prepare the draft of the text and graphics to be included in the brochure. Use clear and simple language. Provide short but descriptive headings and relate these to the overall theme.

Have eye-catching and imaginative graphics. Take help of an artist or computer to prepare graphics or artwork. No brochure is complete without photographs, so ask the organization to provide you relevant photos. Otherwise, organise a photo-shoot with a professional photographer. Infographics can be used to show growth, trends, progress or the achievements of the organisation.

House Journal: A house journal is a periodical journal, which tries to establish regular communication between an organisation, its employees and various other audiences. It is a communication product by large organisations to engage with multiple communities. In the small organisation, the owner calls his employees together and communicates face-to-face, however, in the bigger organisations, direct communication becomes difficult, therefore, messages are conveyed through different and more sophisticated channels. Decades back, an organisation would issue cyclostyled circulars but now these have taken the shape of newsletters and house journals.

An internal house journal creates a sense of belongingness among its employees. It seeks to improve the morale of the employees, build transparency and create a favourable climate for the working of the organisation. It is an instrument for the management to keep the employees posted about the thoughts, plans and activities of the organisation.

Similarly, external communication journals are circulated outside the company or organisation, such as consumers, dealers, retailers, shareholders etc. These are communication products that create visibility for the organisation and open up marketing avenues as well. Such journals are important to create an image of trust, help in brand building as well as keep the general public informed about the new products or services that the company is introducing.

The title of the journal should be short and attractive. It may be more imaginative than descriptive, but such names are difficult to come by. The general tendency is to mention the name or initials of the organisation and add 'news', 'bulletin', 'reporter' or 'newsletter'.

Conference Reports

Publishing the proceedings of a conference, workshop, or a seminar has become an important assignment for a technical writer. Publishing such a document needs care and professional finesse. It also requires several aspects that go beyond just writing the document—writing down the proceedings of the conference, converting it into a readable manuscript, arranging for photographs, interacting with the designer, and finally, seeing the publication through.

The proceedings of the conference should be published as soon as possible otherwise the relevance of the publication is lost. However, there is no one timeline for a conference document to be published because the conferences, seminars, workshops or panel discussions can be of varying durations—ranging from one day to over a week. Also, the nature of conferences can vary from large international conferences to local workshops organised to train a segment of people. It is possible often a photograph and a caption can suffice for a smaller event, while for the bigger conferences a comprehensive document can be published and shared with the participants, the government and other stakeholders.

Irrespective of the size of the event, publishing a conference report is always a challenging task. The organisers and editors are up against a wall in establishing contact with authors who presented their papers and the other participants. Their request to the participants to send their revised papers or to approve their edited documents takes time and necessitates many follow-ups and reminders. Once, this is done, the papers have to be given a uniform style as authors have used different styles of abbreviations, citations and references. More often than not references are missing. Illustrations have to be redrawn. The process takes a long time. Therefore, in order that the process of publishing the proceedings of the conference gets on smoothly, the following steps are suggested:

(i) The technical writer or editor should be a member of the organising committee and should participate in the conference. This will help him plan the publication right from the beginning. Since the editor often has published such proceedings earlier, he should be able to offer proper advice to the organisers from the initial stages itself.

(ii) Some decisions need to be taken before the conference programme is finalised. Such decisions may be: (a) Appointment of the rapporteur for each section/session. (b) The method as to whether the proceedings are to be recorded, transcribed, edited and the facilities available for the jobs in terms of expertise and manpower.

(iii) The form in which papers have to be submitted in advance of the conference. The organising committee should send to the participants rules for typing and preparing the manuscript. The instructions to be sent in this regard: the maximum length of the paper, style of referencing and tables and specifications for illustrations. If these instructions are properly adhered to by the participants, it will make the job of the editor much easier.

(iv) It will help the editor if the manuscripts are submitted well in time. That will give the editor sufficient time to assess the manuscripts and, if need be, get back to the participant for clarification during the conference. This will reduce post-conference discussion and correspondence.

Essential Guidelines for a Technical Writer

We have discussed various kinds of communication products that organisations and companies bring out—Research Bulletins, Special Publications, Research Papers, Handbooks, Manuals, Brochures and House Journals. Each of these products is different and caters to a different audience. It is important for a technical writer to possess a good knowledge of language, and be acquainted with various steps related to designing a publication.

In this section we shall discuss some of those aspects which are essential for converting technical publications into high-class and savvy communication products.

Once a writer or a communication expert has accepted an assignment, he should well remember that he is familiar with various steps in the production of a publication—right from finalising the manuscript till the publication is available. Equally important is that a technical writer ensures that his expertise about various steps that go into making a publication attractive and presentable—illustrations and graphics, designing covers and, of course, presenting statistics in an easy-to-understand way. All this capability will make him an ideal technical and research communicator.

Manuscript Preparation

The manuscript is to be prepared in such a way that it appeals to the organisation and also finds ready acceptance with the publisher. An important element here is to be aware about the readership of the publication. This helps the writer to tailor content according to the needs of the audience.

The next step while writing is to ensure that the draft is complete with details of the event or the product. All the sentences are complete with no spelling or grammatical mistakes. In short, the manuscript should be neat, clear and legible. A well-prepared manuscript means economy for all—the author, publisher and printer. The copy should be such that no further modifications are required during the course of designing and printing.

For this a uniform pattern known as stylization is followed. This means that a particular style is adopted and consistently followed in all matters like punctuation, capitalisation, spellings, abbreviations and connotations. This consistency results in harmony and fineness of presentation. For instance, if we use Twentieth, 20th, and XX, indiscriminately in the same book, and even on the same page, this is bound to create confusion. In this case, it would be appropriate to carry 20th century instead of the other examples. Consistency ensures that the whole book should follow a uniform pattern.

Punctuation, capitalisation, hyphenation and other such particulars should conform to a recognised standard and current usage. Various systems are prevalent, all of which are equally good, and one of these may be followed. The system adopted must be strictly adhered to. To find the same word variously spelt, and punctuation or capitalisation used erratically will be distracting to the reader and will seriously undermine the quality of the publication.

Designing a Publication

Once the text has been finalised and edited, meticulous attention is needed for a proper layout, designing and presentation of the text. The following steps are suggested for designing:

- The photographs, illustrations, graphics and tables should be readied. All of these should have proper captions and these should be properly placed in the text.
- Choose a font family and the various sizes to be used for titles, sub-heads and the body copy. Finalise the colour and shades you plan to use.
- Arrive at an estimate about the number of pages to be printed so that the organisation is aware of the designing and printing costs. You may have to adjust the design according to number of pages and the budget available for the publication.
- Layout is an essential part of the book as it is the first thing that appeals to people. Unless the layout is attractive, people may not utilise or read the book properly. The various components of layout—headings, blurbs, sub-headings, placement of infographics, illustrations/photographs and spaces to be left blank have to be visualised by both the writer as well as the designer.
- For an accurate implementation of the plan, preparing a dummy will help the writer convey the idea about the publication to the printer. Based on this idea, the designer can frame a blue print and discuss with the organisation and the writer.
- Planning the title page is important. In most cases, the designer and the layout artist will make this but the writer will have to verify this to ensure that there are no mistakes.
- Designing the inside cover pages is equally important. The layout artist and the author of the book discuss and decide

about these pages. The name of the publication, author, publisher and that of the institution are given due importance. The purpose of the cover is to attract attention. The cover is what the readers see first.

Illustrations: The term illustration refers to a variety of materials such as drawings, photographs, charts, graphs and maps. The objective of an illustration is to make the subject readily comprehensible. Tables are separately listed in the preliminary pages and separately numbered.

All illustrations should be clear, artistic and meticulously planned so that they convey information effectively to the reader. Like tables, illustrations should also be self-explanatory.

There are various kinds of illustrations—line drawings (diagrams, histograms, graphs) and photographs. Illustrations are referred to in the text as 'Figs' (singular, 'Fig') spelt with capital 'F'. As in case of tables, the illustrations should preferably follow immediately after a reference in the text.

Illustrations should have a purpose. Otherwise, they should not take space. Each illustration should fulfil the following criterion:

I. How does it relate to the author's message?
2. What is its purpose in relation to the text?

Photographs: A photograph constitutes an important part of a publication. Sometimes, the subject matter cannot be made clear without a photograph. Photographs serve two purposes—making sense clear to the reader and making the book interesting and attractive. The quality of a photograph should be excellent, otherwise, the very purpose will be defeated.

Legends to Figures: To explain what a figure is about, legend (title/caption) is placed at its bottom. The legend is preceded by the Figure number (Example: Fig. 10). Legends (like captions of tables) should be concise, self-contained statements of what is presented in the figure.

All figures in a publication should be numbered in consecutive series. The pages containing figures should also be numbered in the same series as those of the text. The page should appear at the same position as on the text pages.

Footnotes to Figures: Symbols used in illustrations, source of illustration (if it is not author's own), special features of illustrations etc. should be explained in footnotes. The first line of the footnote begins one double space below the legend to the figure. The footnotes matter is single-spaced. One double space is left between footnotes.

Layout of Tables

Data collection by the researcher will make sense only if it is presented in a systematic manner. The data is tabulated to get broad characteristics of the subject in an easier to understand manner. Tabulation is a proper arrangement of the data in accordance with classification in proper tabular form facilitating proper analysis. It enables the researcher to simplify the complex data so that comprehension becomes easier.

Tables are used to present extensive numerical data within a short space and with greater clarity. A table should be self-contained and self-explanatory. In no case should a table be used for information which has already been given adequately to present it in textual form rather than tabular form.

The following data does not need to be presented in a tabular form. *A survey of 150 villages in 12 districts of Haryana showed that 349 men and women received various short trainings organised by the Haryana Agricultural University during 1984.*

- All tables should be numbered consecutively in Arabic numerals throughout the manuscript.
- The word TABLE in capitals with its number is centred on the page. If there is text above the table, the table number is placed three spaces below the text.
- The caption is given one double space below the table number. The captions should be short, they should not be followed by a period since these are not complete sentences. Only the first word and proper nouns in caption have capital initials.
- If possible, a table should follow immediately after it is mentioned in the text.
- Always mention the sources of data at the foot of the table.

Placement of Numbers

- Use figures whenever a standard unit of measurement follows a number, for example: 8 kg, 10 ml, 105°C, 5.6 cm, 15 mm and 23 kms.
- Use words up to number nine and figures for all numbers over nine, for example: nine buffaloes, 10 camels, 25 ducks. However, only numbers should be used for a series of experimental data, for example, after 5 days of administering the drug and after 25°C the water will begin to change.
- Never begin a sentence with a number. Either use words in place of numbers or reconstruct the sentence. For example, Eighty-three protestors were arrested.
- Space out numbers if confusion is likely to be caused by the use of figures, for example: fifty 5-day-old chicks were sold to the hotel.
- Spell out all indefinite and approximate periods of time and all other numbers that are used in general manner, for example: about one hundred years ago, thirty years old, three hours, two-and-a-half hours.
- Use figures for all numbers referring to tables.
- Use figures for hours of the day. Separate hours and minutes by a colon, for example: 7:00 hr; 15:30 hr and 12:00 hr.
- Use figures for money preceded by currency symbols, for example: Rs. 25; $ 50, £100.
- Compounds of half and quarter should be joined with hyphens, for example; half-past three, quarter-full petrol.
- Use a comma after every three digits, from right to left in a number of four or more figures in tabular matter, for example: 1,500. In text, however, do not use a comma in a number of four figures, for example: 1500.
- In large numbers, substitute a word for part of the number, for example: 2.5 million and not 2,500,000.
- Use per cent in the text and % in tables. Do not use percentage for per cent.
- As far as possible, avoid use of Roman numerals, as they require more space and are not easily understood. For example: Vol. 34, not Vol. XXXIV.

Style Book

The purpose of the style book is to provide uniform presentation of the printed word. It sets standards for the use of abbreviations, capital letters, titles, punctuation and dates. The style book eliminates arbitrary and haphazard decisions. Several publishing houses, newspapers and news agencies have published useful style books. The Coordinating Committee of Non-Aligned News Agencies Pool published a style book in 1985. It is a useful and handy publication for use by reporters.

A technical communicator should be able to find a stylebook from Indian or international newspapers and magazines as each of the publications follows its own style of writings and spellings. In addition, a good dictionary and a thesaurus are absolutely essential. With the advent of the internet and software applications which are available over smart phones, every journalist and writer should have the app for a dictionary available on his phone.

Citations/References

All references cited should be listed alphabetically, according to the author's surname, on a separate page(s), at the end of the text. The information and style of presentation required in four common types of references is as follows:

Books: Authors(s)/editor(s), year of publication, title of book, place of publication, publisher.

Articles in journals: Author(s), year of publication, title of article, title of periodical (written in full), volume number, issue number (if applicable), page numbers, place of publication.

Articles within books: Author(s), year of publication, title of chapter or article, title of publication, editor(s), place of publication, publisher.

Unpublished Papers Presented at Workshops, Conferences etc.: Author(s), title of paper, title of meeting, sponsoring agency, dates of meeting, location of meeting.

REFERENCES

Ian Montagnes (1991): *Editing and Publishing – Training Manual*, International Rice Research Institute, Manila.

James P. Chapman (1965): *Passing the word – Writing for Publication*, OSU—US Aid Mission, Ludhiana.

UNESCO (1970): *Preparing Text Book Manuscripts, A Guide for Authors in Developing Countries*, Paris.

Usha Raman (2002): Interface between end-user and producer, *The Hindu*, 22 January.

Glossary

ABC Audit Bureau of Circulation. It is entrusted with the responsibility of certifying audited statistics of circulation of a publication.

Accountability This means that a government and its institutions are answerable to the public and the media regarding their performance and responsibilities.

Adversarial approach to journalism A style of reporting that sees news as information needed by the public. It emphasises the watchdog role of the media.

Advertorial A paid advertisement containing advertisements and information that is designed to resemble news.

Advocacy style of journalism A journalistic approach in which the journalist openly advocates or promotes a cause or position.

AFP French news agency—gence France Presse.

Agony column A regular feature in a newspaper or magazine offering advice on personal problems to readers who write letters seeking advice from the newspaper.

Alignment Placing the text in a format that is in a straight line. Alignment of text can be left, right or justified.

Angle An approach to a story or the news peg of a story.

AP Associated Press.

Art Editor A design editor whose job is to design newspapers and magazines with text, photographs, graphics and other designing techniques.

Backgrounder A feature article in a newspaper or a magazine that provides background information about the news.

Banner A headline given to an important news item that stretches across all columns of the page.

Beat An exclusive topic assigned to a reporter is called a beat. Typical beats are the Crime beat, Law beat, Education beat, Health beat, Foreign Affairs beat and many others. Beats are also devised on the basis of geographical areas like a city or region.

Broadsheet Full size newspaper with eight columns which is approximately 22 inches into 15 inches. Sometimes the term broadsheet is denoted for newspapers giving general news as opposed to tabloid newspapers which lay emphasis on crime, celebrity and scandalous type of news.

Byline The name of the reporter or writer who has written a news article or an opinion piece. It establishes the authorship of the writer.

Caption Text given underneath photographs or graphics which describes the photograph, graphics or illustration.

Centre spread The two middle pages in the newspaper which are often used for special reports and important photo-features. It occupies a prominent position in magazines.

Chequebook journalism The practice of paying large amounts of money to celebrities or politicians for publishing their stories. Often reporters pay money to the sources for getting information. Even though it is practiced, it is considered to be an unethical practice.

Circulation The number of copies of a magazine or newspaper sold to readers through subscriptions, sales and post.

Civil Society Organisations and individual who are a part of non-governmental organisations (NGOs), grassroots bodies, advocacy and people's groups that allow for citizen participation. It is a social culture of trust, support and solidarity where people are willing and able to co-operate in advocacy, campaigns and the uplift of the society. A strong civil society is necessary for a thriving democracy.

Classified ads Small advertisements usually taken in single-columns which are displayed according to sections—real estate, business, personal and marriage advertisements.

Column (1) The vertical divisions of a newspaper or a magazine page. A broadsheet newspaper may have eight columns while a tabloid may have just four columns. A magazine may have three to four columns. (2) A periodical article, which is usually an opinion piece, is also called a column. Columns are written by senior journalists or experts on selected topics.

Columnist A writer or journalist who writes an opinion piece on a regular periodical basis, fortnightly or weekly, is called a columnist.

Copy An article or a feature that has been written for publication in a newspaper or magazine but has not been published is called copy.

Copy editing The process of editing an article by doing spelling and grammatical corrections, improving the language and checking factual information. It also involves giving a headline.

Copy editor A journalist who is responsible for editing and improving the copy sent by reporters in a newspaper or magazine. Copy editors also work in publishing houses where they edit manuscripts for books.

Copyright The ownership of original material like an article, a photograph or graphics.

Correspondent A senior reporter is called a correspondent.

Credit line The name of the person who has taken a photograph, created a graphic or made an illustration. The credit line for photographers is the same as a byline for reporters. It establishes the individual's creative ownership on the material created.

Data compression Reducing the size of a file by eliminating unnecessary information and by reducing its quality. It is usually applied to photographs and graphics to make them compatible for websites.

Desk The editorial department in a newspaper or a magazine comprising the Chief Editor, Senior Sub-Editor and Sub-Editors. The responsibility of the Desk includes editing, giving headlines and making layouts for the pages.

Developing news Any news that is taking place continuously and is being reported in real-time is developing news. The coverage of election results, the reporting of a war and generating news from a natural disaster become developing news.

Development journalism A type of journalism in which emphasis is laid on reporting and writing that promotes the cause of human development. Journalists writing on these issues will highlight issues related to education, health, environment and also government policies that lead to the welfare and progress of the people.

Double column News displayed or taken in two columns.

Dummy It is an exact replica of a newspaper or a magazine with proper designing, text and photographs which clearly shows how the newspaper will look after it is published. A dummy is printed so that the journalists working in the organisation get hands on practice of how their publication will look like once it is launched for the public.

Editorial The editor or the newspaper's views on current affairs. The editorials are published on the Edit Page of the newspaper and do not have a byline as these are meant to show the views of the media organisation.

Embargo The time before which a press release cannot be published by journalists but has already been shared with the media. Embargos are issued by PR agencies.

Exclusive A news story which only one journalist and his newspaper has. It could be an investigative news, an interview with a person of importance or any news item that has been obtained by one journalist before any other newspaper or journalist could get it.

Filler A short news story of less importance used to fill up a small space on a newspaper page.

Flash Important but brief news message flashed in pointers or headlines by TV Channels or news agencies. Done when the news is important and is a breaking news.

Follow-up A news or a feature story that is a follow-up of a previous story. A follow-up may uncover new facts or may try to provide additional information in the form of a feature story.

Freebie Free trips, services, entertainment offered to a journalist by Public Relations' companies or governments.

Freelance Self-employed professionals including journalists, who are not in regular employment with organisations or companies.

Gatekeeping The process of selection or rejection of news in media organisations such as newspapers, radio and television. The editor plays an important role in gatekeeping.

Global Village A phrase used to describe ways in which the electronic media and information technologies have created an interconnected world in the fields of media as well as communication.

Graphics Editor A journalist who heads the graphics team comprising illustrators and designers to co-ordinate the production of maps, charts, diagrams, illustrations and info-graphics for news.

Gutter The space between two columns is called the gutter space.

Handout A term used for news release or press release. Corporations, businesses, universities, organizations, political parties, governments and NGOs send handouts to alert the media about their work and activities.

Hard News News that has to be reported in a timely manner otherwise it loses its news value. Events, accidents, speeches are news come under hard news in contrast to feature articles.

Hold Over To keep articles for later use due to constraints of space or if it is a feature article.

House Journal A periodic publication used for providing information and keeping staff informed about its activities. It is a publication edited and published by a company or organisation for internal distribution.

Human Interest Story A news article about human condition or emotional appeal, but is not necessarily hard news. Human interest stories are about individuals and communities that touch upon social issues.

In-depth Story News story that provides a detailed account of a news and goes beyond a basic news story. It will contain extensive research, interviews, background information as well as photographs and info-graphics.

Information Societies Countries where information workers are more in number than occupational categories of people such as farmers, industrial workers, or service workers.

Infotainment The merging of information and entertainment in journalism or mass communication in a bid to make information more captivating for the audience.

Investigative Journalism A form of reporting in which a news story has been researched in depth by a team of reporters. It is a style of reporting that may require months of investigation, fact-finding, interviews and cross-checking of information in order to gain the inside story and expose wrong doing.

Layout The arrangement of text, illustrations and photographs in a newspaper and magazine according to the importance of news.

Lead The most important story in a newspaper which appears on the top of the page.

Manual of style A book of instructions on grammar, spellings, hyphenation and punctuation, which is published by media organisations to ensure that there is consistency in spellings and style in the organisation.

Manuscript The draft of a book or article, before it is sent for printing. Manuscript means 'written by hand,' but the word is now applied to any writing that has not been published.

Marketing Approach to Journalism Approach to journalism that pursues the goal of maximizing profits by selling news as a product, devoting resources to audience research and emphasising on sales and marketing.

Masthead The name or title of a newspaper at the top of page one.

Metro Editor A senior journalist who is the head of the reporting team that is responsible for news coverage in a city. He assigns duties to local reporters.

Mug Shot Photograph showing only a person's face.

New Media Technologies The large-scale developments in the field of communication systems and technologies which have brought about a revolution in the media industry and communication systems. The term is used to refer to cable, satellite, internet technologies as well as other computer and mobile based media.

News Current or fresh information about an important person, event or happening that is gathered, processed and disseminated to a large number of people.

News Agency An organization that collects, edits and distributes news to media organisations such as magazines, newspapers, radio and television channels.

News Editor A senior journalist who heads the desk, supervises copy editors, selects news and decides placement of news stories.

News Process A series of steps from news gathering by reporters to editing of copy to designing pages and dissemination of news to the public.

News Story Write-up or broadcast piece that chronicles who, what, where, when, why and how of a news event.

News Value Criteria used by journalists to judge the newsworthiness, or importance, of a story. Criteria include potential impact of the event on the audience, timeliness, prominence of people involved, geographical proximity of the event to the audience, bizarreness and the degree of conflict.

Nose for News A reporter's instinct, or news sense, which is used to gather information and to make news decisions as quickly as possible.

Op-ed Page Abbreviation for Opposite the Editorial Page. The Op-ed page is devoted to a mix of views and opinion columns.

Paperback A less expensive version of a book that is paperbound and does not have a hard cover.

Personality Profile Feature story that focuses on the personality of a person who is in or out of news. Such articles are good examples of creative writing and paint an interesting, easy-to-read and vivid picture of a person.

Press Release Official announcement by governments, companies and organisations given to the media for use. Also called a handout issued to the media for publication.

Proof The printout of a final page in a newspaper or magazine which is given a last look for errors before it is sent for printing.

Proof Reading The art of carrying out corrections in the proofs.

Proof-reader A person who marks corrections on the proofs and checks for errors before news pages are finally sent for printing.

Pull-out Separate section of a newspaper that can be pulled out, often with separate pagination. These usually come out on weekends and are also called supplements.

Put to Bed When all the pages of a newspaper or magazine have been finalised and the printing press is ready to print.

Reuters International news and photo agency.

Rewrite To write for a second time to strengthen a story or to condense it. Often senior editors on the desk will rewrite the copy sent by a Reporter to improve the readability of the news.

Soft News News stories that focus on human interest, situations, people or events. They can be put in the hold-over for later use. Soft news stories may not be time bound.

Stringer Correspondent of a newspaper who is not on the regular payroll but is paid according to the number of articles and the length of the articles.

Style Rules for capitalization, punctuation and spelling that standardize usage so that the writing style and language is uniform. Most newspapers and stations have stylebooks to ensure that spelling, abbreviation, punctuation and capitalization conform to a certain style. In TV and radio channels, the broadcast stylebooks include pronunciations.

Sub-Editor Person who corrects and edits copy for a newspaper and writes the headlines.

Tabloid A newspaper printed on paper of a special size, which is usually twelve by sixteen inches or five columns wide. Tabloids are almost half in size as compared to the broadsheet newspapers. Tabloids are usually associated with low quality journalism and used to publish sensational or bizarre content. Today tabloids may include newspapers that mix sensationalism with professionalism.

Tailpiece Usually a paragraph with finishing touches, a joke at the end, something added on to enliven a column.

Tele-medicine The practice of using videoconferencing and video calls to diagnose illness and provide medical treatment.

Tip A small bit of information that could lead to the development of a news story.

Trend Story Type of feature story that examines current trends in society and a country.

Wire Service Also called news agency. Some of the Indian wire services are the Press Trust of India (PTI), India Abroad News Service (IANS) while some of the international news agencies are the Associated Press (AP) and the Agence France Presse (AFP).

Yellow Journalism Publications, usually tabloid newspapers, specialising in news that is sensational or grossly exaggerated. Such publications give preference to news such as crime, gossip, celebrities and gossip.

Bibliography

Aggarwal, Vir Bala and V.S. Gupta (2001): *Handbook of Journalism and Mass-Communication*, Concept Publishing Company, New Delhi.

British Council (2001): *A Manual of Human Rights Reporting in India*, Press and People, New Delhi.

Bruce D. Itule and Douglas A. Anderson (1994): *News Writing and Reporting for Today's Media*, McGraw-Hill, Inc. New York.

Dominick, Joseph R. (1990): *The Dynamics of Mass Communication*, McGraw Hill Publishing Company, New York.

Farhat Basir Khan, *The Game of Votes: Visual Media Politics and Elections in the Digital Era*, Sage.

Geoffrey Harris and David Spark (1997): *Practical Newspaper Reporting*, Focal Press, Oxford.

George, T.J.S. (1989): *Editing: A Handbook for Journalists*, Indian Institute of Mass Communication, New Delhi.

Gregory A. Barnes (1986): *Write for Success*, ISI Press, Philadelphia.

Gupta, V.S. and Indu Grover (1996): *Study Material, for the participants in Refresher Course on Communication Skills and Reporting*, Haryana Agricultural University.

Indira Gandhi National Open University (1991): *Writing for Radio-Reaching the Public*, New Delhi.

James M. Neal and Suzanne S. Brown (2000). *Newswriting and Reporting*, The Iowa State University Press.

K.M. Shrivastava, News Reporting and Editing, Sterling Publishers.

Keval J. Kumar, Mass Communication in India, Jaico Publishing House.

Kamath, M.V. (1983): *The Journalist's Handbook*, Vikas Publishing House Pvt. Ltd., New Delhi.

Kamath, M.V., *Professional Journalism*, Vikas Publishing House, New Delhi.

Page, David and Crawley, William (2001): *Satellites Over South Asia*, Sage Publications, New Delhi.

Parthasarathy, Rangaswami (1994): *Here is the News: Reporting for the Media*, Sterling Publisher Pvt. Ltd., New Delhi.

Press Council of India (2001): *Future of Print Media*, New Delhi.

Sainath, P., *Everybody Loves a Good Drought*, Penguin.

Strunk William and E.B. White (1999): *The Elements of Style*, Allyn and Bacon, Massachusetts.

The Media Foundation (1996): *Beyond Those Headlines*, New Delhi.

UNESCO (1970): *Preparing Text Book manuscripts, A guide for authors in developing countries*, Paris.

Index